Making the Connection
Learning Skills Through Literature

Making the Connection
Learning Skills Through Literature

Patricia Pavelka

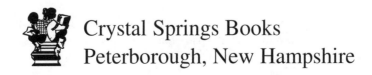

Crystal Springs Books
Peterborough, New Hampshire

©1995 by Patricia Pavelka

Printed in the United States of America
01 00 99   6 5

Published and distributed by:
    Crystal Springs Books
    Ten Sharon Road, Box 500
    Peterborough, NH 03458-0500
    1-800-321-0401

Publisher Cataloging-in-Publication Data

Pavelka, Patricia, 1959- .
        Making the connection : learning skills through literature / Patricia
Pavelka.—1st ed.
[142] p. : ill ; cm.
Includes bibliography and index.
Summary : Part I introduces various instructional approaches and shows how to
develop a print-rich environment for K-2 students. Part II gives examples of how
to use literature to teach specific skills to emergent, developing, and independent readers.
ISBN 1-884548-03-2
1. Reading (Elementary)—Language experience approach. 2. Language experience approach
in education. 3. Language arts (Elementary). I. Title.
371.6 / 4044—dc20   1995   CIP
Library of Congress number: 95-71328

Illustrations and cover design: Phyllis Pittet
Book design: Susan Dunholter
Editor: Deborah Sumner

Dedicated to:

Mom, my best friend;
Paul, my knight in shining armor;
and
Richard, my brother and
inspiration.

Acknowledgments

Thank you to Cheryl Alander for her assistance and encouragement; Kim Couture
for sharing her classroom and expertise with me; Debbie Sumner for her suggestions,
editing expertise and encouragement; Lorraine Walker for her organizational vision
and support; Virginia Moore, the MAC expert, for her guidance and patience;
The Society For Developmental Education family for their support and
especially to Jim Grant, whose belief in me has opened
many doors and made this book a reality.

Table of Contents

Bibliography

INTRODUCTION
Why Literature?

As I reflect upon my sixteen years of teaching in grades kindergarten through four, the one thing that stands out is the difference in how I taught reading when I began and how I view reading instruction now.

When I first began teaching, I used a basal series with three books students had to get through in a year. The series also included language, reading, and phonics workbooks, and a book of blackline masters to run off for children who were having difficulty reading.

My classroom was overflowing with workbooks, reproducibles, blackline masters, and dittos — all of the materials I thought students needed to learn skills. I taught skills in isolation, completely unrelated to the process of reading.

I remember working with my third-grade class on contractions. Students completed many isolated drills on the blackboard and did at least eight to ten workbook and worksheet pages. They all achieved above 85% on their contractions test. I was thrilled. "What a great job teaching contractions," I thought to myself. "I won't need to address this skill again since they have all mastered it."

Was I right?

During the following weeks, I noticed that students were not spelling contractions correctly in their daily writing, nor were they using them properly. One day I became extremely frustrated and said to the class, "I don't know what is wrong with you. You have all achieved A's and B's on the contraction test but are not spelling or using them correctly in your writing." I then went to the board and put up an example of one of their mistakes (dident) and began my loud lecture. Since they had all mastered the skill of contractions, yet were not using them, didn't it follow that they were just being lazy and weren't taking the time?

I'll never forget what happened next. This was the turning point in my career when I knew I had to change. One of my students called out (didn't even raise his hand), "Wait a minute! You mean that 'dident' over there on the board is the same 'didn't' we were learning about in our workbooks?"

I was surprised and could not understand why my students had made no connection between the "didn't" they had studied as a skill and the one they were using in their reading and writing. Teaching skills in isolation was not working!

At that time, I was aware of and familiar with many teaching strategies that process classrooms were using, such as shared reading and language experience stories. But it wasn't until I became aware of this blatant lack of connection on my students' part that I decided to try them.

As I started moving away from commercial programs towards children's literature, I was concerned about accountability. How could I make sure I was teaching the needed skills at my grade level if I didn't have a basal program to follow? How were my students going to learn skills if they didn't have workbooks to practice them in?

I began looking for books that were good models for teaching specific reading and writing skills. At first this seemed like an overwhelming task. But I took one skill at a time. When I knew we were going to be involved in a lesson on quotation marks, I began looking for books, poems, and chants that used quotation marks abundantly. As my students discussed using quotation marks, we looked at many examples of how they were used in meaningful contexts, rather than just putting isolated sentences on the board.

Next, I thought about what students could do instead of completing numerous workbook pages and dittos. Assignments started to become more meaningful to students rather than just isolated practice. For example, instead of students doing two workbook pages of reading sentences and circling what was being said and then two dittos of putting in quotation marks, they were writing conversations between two characters such as Frog and Toad (see page 91). They were also interviewing each other, writing down responses, and reporting to the class. They were actively involved in the learning process and applying what they were learning to their reading and writing.

The Difference I've Observed

During the past few years the change I have seen in my students' motivation, interest, and achievement has been incredible. As I compare what was happening in my classroom then and what is happening now, I first thought about my students:

THEN	NOW
unmotivated	motivated
uninterested	interested
saw little meaning in reading and writing	see reading and writing as a means of communicating and a form of enjoyment
could not transfer skills	apply skills in meaningful contexts
were schooltime readers	are readers in and out of school
unsure	confident, high self-esteem
not risk takers	risk takers
majority of time spent on paperwork	majority of time spent on reading
did not talk about or share books	constantly sharing and borrowing books from each other

I also thought about the materials we were using:

THEN	NOW
uninteresting	interesting
skills taught in isolation	skills taught in meaningful contexts
contrived language	predictable, natural language
meaning was not a priority	meaning dominates
phonics and skills were the heart of the program	comprehension and meaning are the heart of the program
levels	no levels
dull illustrations	beautiful illustrations
enormous amounts of paperwork	meaningful extensions
story elements kept to a minimum	story elements fully developed

A Place to Begin

Making the Connection: Learning Skills Through Literature is the result of what I went through when making the change to a process classroom where students are actively involved in meaningful learning activities.

I believe that as teachers use the ideas presented here they will begin to see a change in students' motivation, interest, and achievement and, at the same time, feel they are effectively teaching the skills their curriculum demands.

Part I: Teaching Through Meaningful Contexts explains in detail the different instructional approaches I began to use and the skills that can be addressed through each approach.

It also looks at characteristics of students as readers and writers and of reading materials appropriate for children at the emergent, developing, and independent stages of reading development.

As I began finding books that were good models for skills and began developing meaningful activities to go along with them, I needed a place to organize this information. I created a planning guide, which is explained in detail on page 29.

Part II: Teaching Skills Through Literature is the compilation of the planning sheets I created. Skills can be found in alphabetical order and are appropriate for students at the three stages of reading development.

Although I give very specific skills, literature, and activities to use, they are not meant to be the "end all, be all." I developed them based on the needs of my students and curriculum. Many of these may be appropriate for you. If so, please use them, but it is also important for you to find good literature and develop skills lessons that will meet the specific needs of *your* students and curriculum. That is where you will find the planning guide most helpful.

Part I
Teaching Through
Meaningful Contexts

Creating a Print-rich Environment

Children learn more by what we do than what we say. It's like that old saying: Practice what you preach.

If we are *telling* our students that reading and writing are important, that we place a high value on those two things, we also have to *show* them!

Put poems and chants on charts and hang them up for students to see. Post directions for art projects or center instructions. Put name tags on cubbies, lockers, coat hooks, desks, or tables. Use labels and signs to designate centers and to show where materials such as scissors, glue, and paper belong. Prominently display children's work. Each day, write and display morning messages and language experience stories.

PRINT IS EVERYWHERE!

Classroom Libraries

Libraries should be inviting, cozy places for students. Prominently display books with the front cover showing. Feature different books each week or every other week. Have rugs, cushions, pillows, bean bag chairs, couches, oversized chairs, etc., available for comfortable, relaxed reading.

Display books at many different reading levels to accommodate the range of reading abilities in the classroom. There must be books easy enough for all children to read so they feel successful and confident. A variety of reading materials, including fiction, nonfiction, magazines, joke books, newspapers, and books written by students, should be available.

Students see that teachers value reading when libraries and books are the focus of the classroom.

Reading should be the work, not what is done when the work is completed.

In the photo on page 6, books are displayed with covers showing. On the right is a big book display area with hard covers opened up and featured on the top. On the floor to the left, a rack from a card store serves as a great place to feature magazines. Big books written by students are on the back right bulletin board.

Exemplary Classroom Libraries

Books are prominently displayed with the covers out.

Space is large enough for many students to stretch out while reading.

Books are categorized in tubs according to subjects:
    monsters
    friends
    holidays
or authors.

Areas look cozy and inviting.

Instructional Approaches

Retelling

Retelling stories:
- **Helps children internalize story language.**

    Once upon a time . . . .
    They lived happily ever after . . . .
    They gnashed their terrible teeth and they roared their
        terrible roars . . . .
    They went out to seek their fortune . . . .

- **Increases comprehension of stories (beginning, middle, and end)**

- **Helps children internalize story elements (characters, setting, plot, theme, climax)**

    As children have many encounters with retelling, they learn to begin their stories with an introduction of the characters and the setting. They continue with the initial problem or events and retell the events/episodes in order. The idea of a story having a beginning (introduction), middle (series of events/episodes), and end (resolution) becomes internalized. Students begin to organize their thoughts and put the story into a coherent form.

- **Encourages confidence in speaking.**

    I notice the more often my students retell stories, the greater their confidence and self-esteem. For some children, speaking in front of a class is very scary. Have students start out by retelling aloud with no audience, then to a small group, and, finally, to the whole class.

- **Can be used as an assessment tool.**

    Listening to a child retell a story is a quick, easy way to assess whether a student has understood the general, overall meaning of the story. How many details did the child include? Did s/he use story language? Is the retelling organized?

- **Aids in vocabulary growth and expands and develops oral language.**

Individual Storyboards

Storyboards are a way of retelling where students re-create the setting and make paper puppets. There are a number of ways for students to make their own storyboards. Here are three of my students' favorites:

Paper Bag Storyboards

Each student will need his/her own paper bag. Holding the bag either horizontally or vertically, students illustrate the setting on the front of the bag. Students love this because the storyboard stands up while they are retelling. Puppets can be made out of paper and put on popsicle sticks.

Another way to use paper bags is to cut them into the shape of a house, step 1. Staple on two paper doors, step 2. Students can then have two scene settings from the story, one on the doors and one inside the house. Puppets can be kept in back of the storyboard in the pocket that is formed when the doors are stapled on.

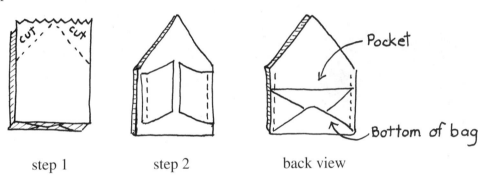

step 1   step 2   back view

Stand up Storyboards

Stand up storyboards can be made with a 9" x 12" piece of paper. If desired, cut the top of the paper into some kind of design, step 1. The paper can also be left alone so that it is rectangular in shape. I found that my students liked the idea of making the top different shapes. Fold the paper into thirds, step 2. Students can now draw the setting. Tape or glue a pocket onto the back of the 9" x 12" paper to hold the puppets.

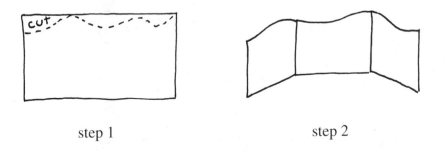

step 1   step 2

Class Storyboards

Class storyboards are used the same way individual storyboards are used; however, they are much larger so that a number of children can work together. These large storyboards can be made from a variety of materials: poster board, mural paper, and boxes. The pictures show some different ways to make class storyboards.

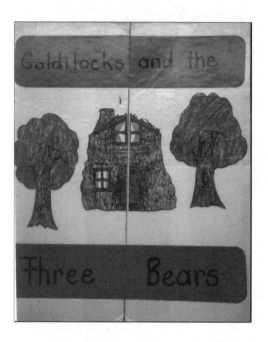

Use the boxes that big books are shipped in. They usually open down the middle and are a ready-made, stand up background for a large storyboard. This box is covered with white contact paper and is the setting for *The Three Bears*. The picture on the left shows the outside of the box while the picture below shows the inside of the box when opened. Puppets are kept in a pocket on the back of the box.

In the story *The Gingerbread Boy*, a boy runs away from his mother. This storyboard is made from two pieces of poster board taped together. It shows the different stops the gingerbread boy made while running away. The gingerbread boy is a figure made out of paper and laminated so students can move him around.

Students painted the scenery on a large piece of mural paper for *Blueberries for Sal*. Sal, her mother, the mother bear and baby bear are all made out of oaktag and laminated. Notice the blueberries on the mural. These are blue plastic lacing objects. Blue pompoms also work well.

Both of these storyboards, *The Three Little Pigs* and *Caps for Sale,* were made out of a big book shipping box. The setting was drawn right on the box with crayons. Some of the items in the picture (fire and pot) were cut out of paper and glued on.

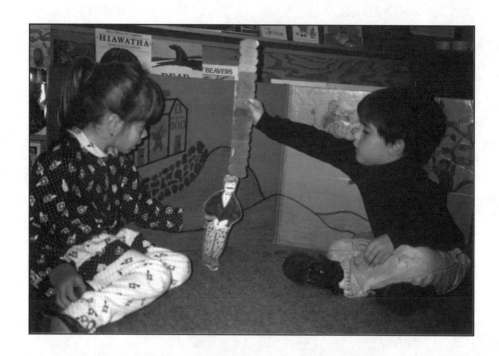

The Tortoise and the Hare storyboard is also made out of a big book shipping box. It is covered with white contact paper and the illustrations are done with crayons and markers. The trees and shrubs were stapled onto toilet paper and/or paper towel tubes.

This *Three Billy Goats Gruff* storyboard is made out of paper bags and 9" x 12" construction paper. The bridge is made of three pieces of paper taped together.

Puppets

Puppets can be made out of small paper bags, socks, paper plates, paper, and popsicle sticks, etc. There are also many commercially made puppets available.

Props

Students retell the story of *The Very Hungry Caterpillar*. They are holding up pieces of food that the hungry caterpillar eats. Notice each piece of food has a hole cut out of the middle. As the story is retold, the caterpillar literally eats through the food.

Masks

Students retell the story of *The Three Billy Goats Gruff* using masks. Masks can also be made out of paper plates or construction paper. Students who are uncomfortable wearing masks can wear headbands instead.

Language Experience

Language Experience teaches reading and writing skills through student-generated texts. Because students use their own experiences and language, the reading material is motivating and interesting. They observe that thoughts can be expressed in language, and language can be recorded and read back. With this approach, both composing and reading are modeled. A first-grade class created the following language experience story after a trip to a farm.

We went to the farm today. We saw a lot of different animals.
We saw pigs, cows, horses, goats, and ducks. The ducks were
quacking at us. One tried to eat Jim's sandwich.

Morning Message

Morning Message is a message/letter that is written to the class each morning. For example:

Dear Kindergartners,
Good morning. You have gym this morning. We are going to read a
very funny story today. It is going to be very hot outside today!

> *Love,*
> *Mrs. Pavelka*

After writing a language experience story or a morning message, students come up to the easel and circle words they know. They can find words that sound alike at the beginning, words that rhyme, sight words, etc.

Skills addressed by language experience stories and morning message:

1. Sight vocabulary
2. Conventions of print
   punctuation
   capital letters
3. Reading/writing
   connection
4. Spelling patterns
   and rhyming
   words
5. Nature and purpose
   of print
6. Each printed word
   represents a
   spoken word
7. Differences among
   letters, words, and
   sentences
8. Word identification
   use of the three
   cueing systems
   (see next page)

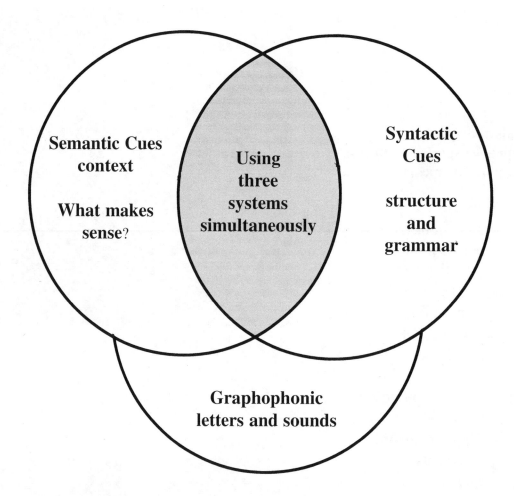

When students come to words they do not recognize by sight, they must have some strategies for figuring out the unknown words. Knowing how to use the three cueing systems gives students strategies to use when encountering unknown words.

> **Semantic cues**: Refer to meaning. What would make sense?
>   Students use context to figure out unknown word.
> **Syntactic cues**: The grammatical structure of our language
> **Graphophonic cues**: Letter and sound correspondence

What word(s) would fit in the sentence below?
   I threw a _____ for my dog to catch.
The words ball, tennis ball, frisbee, stick, branch, and bone would all fit in the blank if we were using both syntactic and semantic cues. But what if the sentence looked like this?
   I threw a f_____ for my dog to catch.
Now my choices are limited because the graphophonic cueing system has been added.

Some students have difficulty reading because of too much emphasis on one cueing system.

Shared Big Book Approach

Components of the shared book approach and skills addressed by each:

1. The teacher reads the book
   Skills addressed:
   - A. Reading is a meaning-making process
   - B. Modeling of fluent reading

2. Pointing to each word as you read
   Skills addressed:
   - A. Directionality: reading goes top to bottom, left to right
   - B. Each printed word represents a spoken word
   - C. Differences among letters, words, and sentences
   - D. Letter/sound relationships

3. Masking is used to focus attention on details of print. An index card or a piece of oaktag is used to cover words, parts of words, or letters.
   Skills addressed:
   - A. Word identification: use of the three cueing systems
   - B. Spelling patterns and rhyming words
   - C. Predicting

4. Repeated reading of the book
   Skills addressed:
   - A. Sight vocabulary (multiple exposures)
   - B. Word identification: use of the three cueing systems
   - C. Comprehension
   - D. Conventions of print: punctuation, capital letters
   - E. Confidence in ability to read

Reading Aloud

"The single most important activity for building the knowledge required for eventual success in reading is reading aloud to children."

Becoming a Nation of Readers:
The Report of the Commission on Reading

Why Read Aloud?
- Promotes concept and language development
- Enhances vocabulary development
- Builds familiarity with story language and story patterns
- Models skillful oral reading
- Creates lifetime readers, not just schooltime readers
- Creates a positive attitude toward reading
- Motivates children to read
- Improves listening comprehension
- Stimulates the imagination
- Establishes the reading/writing connection

Sight Vocabulary

Sight vocabulary refers to printed words that students see and can recognize immediately, without any analysis. A sight vocabulary develops and grows over a period of time because of multiple exposure to words. As students see words in many different contexts, they begin to recognize the words instantly. Think about the first words children learn at sight — McDonald's, STOP, their name. These words are not high frequency words, nor have they been taught by drill. Children have learned them because they are personally meaningful and have been repeatedly exposed to them.

There are two views for developing sight vocabulary when thinking about classroom instruction. Many commercial materials look at lists of high frequency words and then choose only a few words to introduce at a time. Words are presented several times in the text in attempting to make it part of a child's sight vocabulary. Because only a few high frequency words are presented a number of times, reading often becomes unnatural and highly contrived. This view assumes that a child needs to have a repertoire of sight words before s/he can construct meaning from text.

The other view for developing a sight vocabulary is that meaning comes first. Students will acquire a sight vocabulary as a result of meaningful reading experiences. This is what I believed; however, I was concerned about accountability. I wanted to use quality children's literature as the basis for sight vocabulary development and also make sure children were learning the words.

If children develop a sight vocabulary over time because of multiple exposure to words, I needed to look for that repetition in the books I used. For example, I took the book *Brown Bear Brown Bear, What Do You See?* by Bill Martin Jr. and listed all of the high frequency words found in it. I then counted the number of times each word was repeated. I did the same for the book *As I Was Walking Down the Road* by Sarah E. Barchas. The results are shown on the next page.

After the children and I read a big book story together, we go back and look at each page. We can do a number of different activities that focus on sight vocabulary. We use highlighting tape to highlight the sight vocabulary words that I have chosen to concentrate on. Or, I cover the pages with clear contact paper and students circle the words. Sometimes I write five or six sentences from the story on strips of paper and ask students to find a specific sight word in those sentences. When we're done focusing on that word, we go back to the beginning of the story, count, and tally the number of times it appears.

I also put the sight vocabulary word cards in an envelope in the front of the big book. During their independent worktime, students can take the book into the library and "play school" by matching the cards to the words that appear on the pages. Through these experiences, they get repeated practice with the words. I do individual checks with my students three times a year to assess what words they know instantly by sight.

In order to make sure you address all the sight words expected at your grade level, make a copy of the list and check off each word every time you focus on it. The Fry instant word lists for grades one and two (see pages 22, 23) are examples of grade-appropriate words.

Sight Word	Number of times it appears
what	13
do	13
you	13
see	24
I	10
a	20
looking	12
at	12
me	12

Brown Bear, Brown Bear, What Do You See?
by Bill Martin Jr.

Sight Word	Number of times it appears
I	69
was	13
the	6
then	13
saw	11
a	26
little	10
caught	11
it	33
up	13
picked	11

As I Was Walking Down the Road
by Sarah E. Barchas

First 100 Instant Words

(approximately first-grade difficulty)

the	at	there	some	my
of	be	use	her	than
and	this	an	would	first
a	have	each	make	water
to	from	which	like	been
in	or	she	him	called
is	one	do	into	who
you	had	how	time	oil
that	by	their	has	its
it	words	if	look	now
he	but	will	two	find
was	not	up	more	long
for	what	other	write	down
on	all	about	go	day
are	were	out	see	did
as	we	many	number	get
with	when	then	no	come
his	your	them	way	made
they	can	these	could	may
I	said	so	people	part

Reprinted with permission of Edward Fry, author of *Spelling Book Words Most Needed Plus Phonics for Grades 1-6*, Laguna Beach Educational Books, Laguna Beach, CA.

Second 100 Instant Words

(approximately second-grade difficulty)

over	name	boy	such	change
new	good	following	because	off
sound	sentence	came	turned	play
take	man	want	here	spell
only	think	show	why	air
little	say	also	asked	away
work	great	around	went	animals
know	where	form	men	house
place	help	three	read	point
years	through	small	need	page
live	much	see	land	letters
me	before	put	different	mother
back	line	end	home	answer
give	right	does	us	found
most	too	another	move	study
very	means	well	try	still
after	old	large	kind	learn
things	any	must	hand	should
our	same	big	picture	American
just	tell	even	again	world

Reprinted with permission of Edward Fry, author of *Spelling Book Words Most Needed Plus Phonics for Grades 1-6*, Laguna Beach Educational Books, Laguna Beach, CA.

Teaching to Students' Needs

Our students are at different stages of development as readers and writers. Knowing where they have been and where they are going will help us create appropriate goals for them.

Characteristics of Emergent Readers and Writers

- understand the basic grammatical structure of the English language
- know the difference between print and pictures
- know that print carries the story
- use memory and pictures to "read" a story
- can imitate the reading and writing processes
- understand the nature and purpose of print
        know that print carries a message
        know that print represents meaning
- show an interest in print
- begin to understand print concepts
        beginning and ending of a book
        directionality: left to right, top to bottom, return sweep
        one printed word represents one spoken word
        differences among letters, words, and sentences
        word segmentation
- understand some letter/sound correspondence
- recognize some environmental print
- recognize some names

Characteristics of Developing Readers and Writers

- give text more importance than picture cues
- have mastered print concepts
- have mastered letter/sound correspondence (consonants)
- begin to recognize vowel patterns and combinations
- are developing a sight vocabulary
- begin to utilize the three cueing systems
        can use syntax and meaning to predict
        can use initial letter/sound correspondence to predict and confirm
- have knowledge of simple structural analysis
        can recognize most commonly used affixes (ing, ed, s)
        can recognize compound words

- understand conventions such as punctuation and capital letters at beginning of sentences
- know that reading always makes sense
    read for meaning
- begin to read silently
- use inventive spelling
    audience can read what has been written

Characteristics of Independent Readers and Writers

- recognize the majority of words at sight
- read with fluency
- use the three cueing systems simultaneously
- self-correct to gain meaning
- adjust meaning of words according to the context in which they are used
- read silently
- make inferences independently
- draw conclusions independently
- read to learn (informational books)
- fully understand story elements
- begin to rely on visual cues for spelling rather than auditory cues
- can write using a variety of different forms
- read a wide range of different genres

Characteristics of Reading Materials

Emergent

- short and predictable
- repetitive
- use natural language
- use rhyme and rhythm
- simple texts, easy to memorize
- pictures and text closely matched
- illustrations play a major role on each page

Developing

- longer
- more complex
- wide range of vocabulary
- text rather than illustrations play a more important role on each page

Independent

- illustrations are at a minimum
- vocabulary becomes increasingly challenging
- children need to infer meaning from the story
- more characters are introduced and developed
- story elements are more fully developed
- language challenges are introduced (metaphors, similes)
- chapters appear

Use Quality Children's Literature as the Heart of Your Skills Instruction.

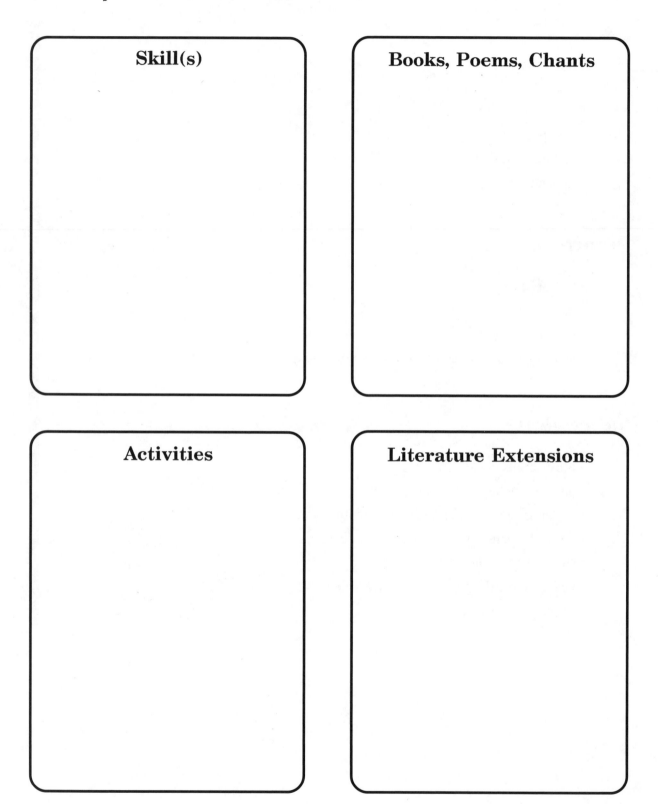

Skill(s)

Books, Poems, Chants

Activities

Literature Extensions

The Planning Guide

I created and designed this planning guide to help organize my thoughts and ideas. It lets me see what books, poems, chants, etc., are good models for certain skills and what activities and literature extensions can be done. I keep these planning guides in a notebook with skills listed in alphabetical order. This makes it easier to find a certain skill quickly when I want to add to it.

The more you work with this planning guide, the more manageable and easier it becomes. Many times I would not be thinking about trying to find a certain poem or book for a skill, but it just happened. I'd be looking at some poems or pick up a new book to read, and the skills just jumped out at me. I would go back to my planning guides and add the new resource.

The planning guide is divided into four sections:

Books, Charts, and Poems

I list the books, chants, and poems that are good models for teaching certain skills.

Skills

I list the skill(s) that I will be working on when using the books, chants, and poems. Many times certain resources are excellent models for teaching a number of different skills. When this happens, I make a separate planning sheet for each skill and add the sheets alphabetically to my notebook.

I usually include sight vocabulary here. The words I choose to focus on are the ones that appear most frequently in the text (see page 20). When I first started choosing words, I actually did a tally like the one shown on page 21 for each book. As I worked more with this format, I was able to get away from the tallies. You may also want to tally the words as you begin doing this.

Activities

What activities will you be doing to help students acquire the skill(s) you are working on? I usually do this in a whole or small group setting. If I am using a big book, I usually do a shared reading experience (see page 19). I also try to use interactive charts as much as possible.

Literature Extensions

What kinds of activities can students do to extend and enrich their interaction with the book and the skill? Students complete most of the extension activities independently. I usually have students do some kind of writing activity.

How to Use the Planning Guide

You can fill out the planning guide in one of two ways:
>   A. Choose a book you like and then find a skill that is
>   embedded in the text (see page 31).
>
>   or
>
>   B. Choose the skill you want to introduce and then find books, chants, and
>   poems that can teach the skill in meaningful context (see page 35).

I use both approaches in filling out the guides. For example, *Polar Bear, Polar Bear, What Do You Hear?* by Bill Martin Jr. is one of my favorites. I wrote down the name of the book first and then proceeded to look for any skills that I could address using it.

Another time I knew I wanted to work on days of the week with my students. I chose that skill first and then looked for reading materials that were good models.

Use Quality Children's Literature
as the Heart of Your Skills Instruction.

---

1 Books, Chants, Poems

Polar Bear, Polar Bear, What Do You Hear?
by Bill Martin Jr.

---

2 Skill(s)

Ending "ing"

Long e sound
me, see, green, sheep, ear, hear

3 Sight Vocabulary
what, do, you, hear, in, my, ear

---

4 Activities

Shared book

Interactive chart:
ee, ea words
jumping (verb+ing)

Cut apart sentences

Match pictures of animals to words

---

5 Literature Extensions

Class Big Books:
Name, Name, What Do You Hear?

Science Topic: What do you see/hear?

Individual books:
I hear a _____ roaring in my ear.

---

1 (Books Chants Poems)

This is a favorite book of mine. Students just love it. So the first thing I did was to write down the name of the book.

5 (Literature Extensions)

These are some extensions that can be done to reinforce the skills using the format of *Polar Bear, Polar Bear.*

---

2 (Skills)

After choosing the book *Polar Bear Polar Bear, What Do You Hear?*, I looked for skills that the book addresses in its text. I found that every verb in this book has an "ing" ending, so I chose that as one skill to work on. There are also many words that have a long e sound, so I chose the "ee" and "ea" patterns to work on.

3 (Sight Vocabulary)

I looked for words that appeared a number of times in the book.

4 (Activities)

These are some activities that can be done to reinforce the skill.

Use Quality Children's Literature as the Heart of Your Skills Instruction.

1 Skill(s)

Days of the week

3 Sight Vocabulary

on, there, was, everywhere, the

2 Books, Chants, Poems

Cookie's Week
by Cindy Ward

4 Activities

Shared book

Interactive chart:
Put days of week in order

Match days of the week with Cookie's adventures.

Give seven students a day of the week card to hold. Have students line themselves up in order.

5 Literature Extensions

Rewrite *Cookie's Week* with Cookie having different adventures.

Students can each write their own book about their pet. How might their pet get into trouble during the week? (Could also be done as a class book. Each page would be a different child and his/her animal. See page 64.)

---

1 (Skills)

Our curriculum had days of the week as a skill my students needed to know. The first thing I did was to write down that skill.

3 (Sight Vocabulary)

I looked for words that appear a number of times in the book.

4 (Activities)

These are some activities that can be done to reinforce the skill.

2 (Books Chants Poems)

The second thing I did was to think about books that include the days of the week. I chose *Cookie's Week*.

5 (Literature Extensions)

These are some extensions that can be done to reinforce days of the week using the format of *Cookie's Week*.

Part II
Teaching
Skills Through
Literature

In most of our K-2 classrooms, we have students at the emergent, developing, and independent stages of reading development. Some skills in this section are suggested for one, two, or all three stages of reading. Please keep in mind that these are only suggestions! Because of the wide range of abilities in classrooms, whether you have a multiage classroom or not, students will master skills at different times. As they are exposed to skills, some students may grasp and master them immediately, while for others, the lesson will be more of an introduction. These students will need further exposure and practice to make the skills their own.

I want students to be able to focus their attention on the skill I am teaching instead of dealing with a difficult text. That's why some books listed in this section may seem easy for students at the developing or independent stages of reading.

I may, for example, teach all my first graders a skill at the emergent level and then plan follow-up lessons for certain students who can handle more difficult reading material. I've organized this section by skill so readers can more easily find appropriate lessons geared toward different levels.

Skills Are Important But...

"Children learn what we teach them. If the literature-based reading program is really a skills-based reading program, they will learn that literature is to be used to learn so-called reading skills, not to make music."
Nancie Atwell
Side by Side

When using these beautiful pieces of children's literature, poems, and chants, make sure you first hear the music. As you read them with your students, laugh, cry, sympathize, and get angry with the characters. Talk about the characters and the setting. Discuss the plot. Have students brainstorm what might have happened if . . . .

After reading for the sheer pleasure and enjoyment of it, revisit the text and begin to look for skills you can teach.

Please help your students hear the music!

Capitalization:
Names of People

(Characters)

EMERGENT
→ **DEVELOPING**
INDEPENDENT

*Tacky
the
Penguin*
by Helen Lester

Tacky is a penguin who lives with five other penguins who are very well mannered and very much alike. Tacky is different.

Activities

List names of all characters in the book: Goodly, Lovely, Angel, Neatly, Perfect, and Tacky. Point out that they begin with capital letters. Find these names throughout the book and look for the capital letters.

Have students look through other books they are reading and find names of some characters. Students can come up to the board and write down the characters' names.

Have students brainstorm some sentences with names in them and write them on the board.

 Other suggested resources:

It's So Nice to Have a Wolf Around The House by Harry Allard
Where the Sidewalk Ends by Shel Silverstein ("Helping," page 101)
It's Mine by Leo Lionni
Three Cheers for Tacky by Helen Lester

Literature Extensions

Have students take a couple of pieces of 8½" by 11" paper and staple them together to make a book. Students can create/decorate their own covers. Put all of the blank books in a box or on a counter. Students now pick any book other than their own and write a message that includes the name of a person, pet, character, etc. They continue doing this until they have written a message in all of the books.

Example:

To help them keep track, give students a class list to check off the names as they write in a book.

Capitalization:
Days of the Week and Holidays

EMERGENT

DEVELOPING

→ **INDEPENDENT**

"I Must Remember"
from *Where the Sidewalk Ends*
by Shel Silverstein

This poem tells about all the things people eat during different holidays. The character in this poem has overeaten!

Activities

Have students brainstorm all the holidays they can think of and write them on the board.

Thanksgiving
Christmas
Kwanzaa
Hanukkah
Easter
Passover
Halloween
Fourth of July
St. Patrick's Day, etc.

Point out the capital letters.

Go back over each one and see if students can tell you about them.

Talk about the things they might eat during the different holidays.

Literature Extensions

Make holiday books. Students can pick three to five holidays from the brainstormed list. Have them write the following about each holiday:

Describe it: date, why it is a special day, etc.

Tell what their family usually does during the holiday.

What foods do they usually eat?

Capitalization:
People, Addresses

EMERGENT

DEVELOPING

➔ **INDEPENDENT**

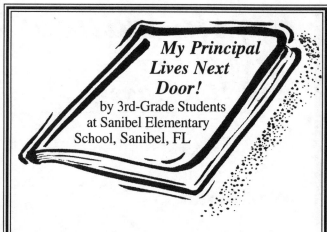

My Principal Lives Next Door!
by 3rd-Grade Students
at Sanibel Elementary
School, Sanibel, FL

Benjamin lives next door to his principal and is not very happy about it. By the end of the story, he realizes it's not so bad.

Activities

List all of the words that are capitalized in the story. Categorize them.

Names of People	Names of Schools
Benjamin James Johnson, Jeff, Betsy, Suzanne, Mr. Meyer, Mrs. Strictly	Hennessey Elementary
Names of Streets	**Names of Cities and States**
Bright Oak Drive	Hennessey, Tennessee

Have students brainstorm other things they can add to each category and write them in the appropriate squares.

Literature Extensions

Have students write about the adventures they might have if they lived next door to the principal or teacher.

This book is published by Willowisp Press, Inc. for the Kids Are Authors Competition. For more information, write to:

SBF Services, Inc.
Kids Are Authors Competition
10100 SBF Drive
Pinellas Park, FL 34666

Cause and Effect

→ **EMERGENT**
DEVELOPING
INDEPENDENT

The Day Jimmy's Boa Ate the Wash
by Trinka Hakes Noble

This is an imaginative cumulative tale about what happens the day a first-grade class goes on a field trip to a farm.

Activities

Have students brainstorm the sequence of events pointing out the causes (C) and effects (E).

E— the cow cried
C— the haystack fell on her

E— the haystack fell
C— the farmer crashed his tractor into it

E— the tractor crashed
C— the farmer was yelling at the pigs

E— the farmer yelled at pigs
C— pigs were on the bus

Discuss how each incident/action is related to the one before and after.

Other suggested resources:

If You Give a Moose a Muffin
by Laura Joffe Numeroff
Jimmy's Boa and the Big Splash Birthday Bash by Trinka Hakes Noble

Literature Extensions

Students can make their own cause-and-effect movies using calculator tape. Have them illustrate the story by making separate frames/ pictures for each cause and effect. Roll up the paper and tape a pencil onto each end.

Cause and Effect

EMERGENT
➡ **DEVELOPING**
INDEPENDENT

If You Give a Mouse a Cookie
by
Laura Joffe Numeroff

This is a story about all of the things that could happen if you give a mouse a cookie.

Activities

Make a cause-and-effect map of the story.

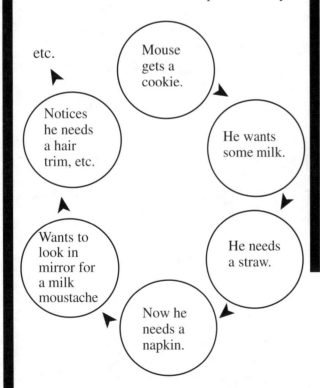

etc.

Mouse gets a cookie.

He wants some milk.

He needs a straw.

Now he needs a napkin.

Wants to look in mirror for a milk moustache

Notices he needs a hair trim, etc.

Use either sentence strips or pieces of paper to write on. You can write these ahead of time or with students as you are doing the activity.

Literature Extensions

Students can make their own versions of *If You Give a Mouse a Cookie.*

If You Give a Mouse a Hammer . . . .

If You Give a Mouse a Slice of Pizza . . . .

If You Give a Mouse a Bicycle . . . .

or

They can start with a new beginning.

If You Give an Elephant a _____ . . . .

If You Give a Guinea Pig a _____ . . . .

If You Give a Teacher a _____ . . . .

Cause and Effect

EMERGENT

DEVELOPING

➜ **INDEPENDENT**

The Steadfast Tin Soldier
by Hans Christian Anderson

A one-legged tin soldier falls in love with a paper dancer. He has many scary and exciting adventures.

Activities

Brainstorm with students all of the causes and effects in the story. Talk about how one action or event causes other actions and events to happen.

Make a cause-and-effect mural with text and/or illustrations.

CAUSE	EFFECT
When the last soldier was molded, there wasn't enough tin left.	The last soldier had one leg.
The dancer had her leg raised so high in the air the tin soldier could not see it.	The tin soldier thought she had only one leg like him.
The tin soldier was placed on the window sill.	The window swung open and the tin soldier fell out.

Literature Extensions

Students can write about different effects that could have stemmed from certain events such as:

There wasn't enough tin left to mold a whole soldier so the last soldier:

> had one arm
> was never made
> was made shorter and smaller

. . . the window suddenly swung open, and out fell the tin soldier:

> into a river or lake.
> into a car.
> onto the limb of a tree.

What other things might have been different in the story if these causes and effects were changed?

Character Development

→ **EMERGENT**

DEVELOPING

INDEPENDENT

Nora is a mouse who has a brother and a sister. She tries to get her parents' attention by doing all sorts of things.

Sight Vocabulary

then	said
Nora	she

Activities

Talk about the main character, Nora. Have students describe her and then back up their opinion with things that happened in the story. Write down their responses.

> impatient — kept doing things so her parents would pay attention to her now

> naughty — slammed the door, dropped her sister's marbles on the floor

 Other suggested resources:

Sylvester and the Magic Pebble
   by William Steig
The Little Red Hen
Corduroy by Don Freeman
The Gingerbread Boy by Paul Galdone

Literature Extensions

Make a character poster using the information brainstormed during the activity. Each child can choose a trait of Nora's and illustrate what happened in the book to verify that trait.

Have students make a character poster of themselves.

Character Development

EMERGENT
➡ **DEVELOPING**
INDEPENDENT

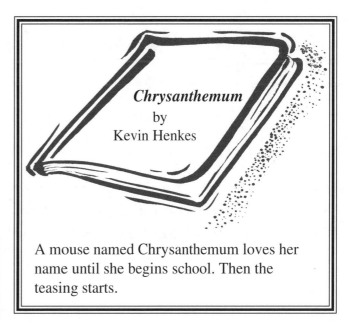

Chrysanthemum
by
Kevin Henkes

A mouse named Chrysanthemum loves her name until she begins school. Then the teasing starts.

Activities

Talk about the changes in self-confidence that Chrysanthemum goes through. Chart her highs and lows. (Use yarn to make the graph.)

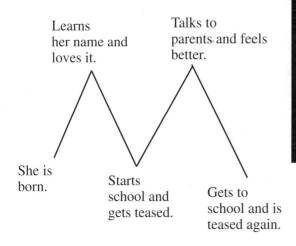

Learns her name and loves it.

Talks to parents and feels better.

She is born.

Starts school and gets teased.

Gets to school and is teased again.

On sentence strips, write all of the events and happenings that led to the rise and fall of her self-esteem.

Literature Extensions

Have students interview their parents and find out how and why they received their names. Students can draw pictures of themselves and tell about their names. Put them all together in a class book.

Have students think about events in their own lives that made them happy and sad and make graphs of their feelings. The graphs can start when they were born and end with today. Give students pieces of colored yarn and white paper to make the graphs.

The character maps on pages 44 and 46 are good to use as an extension with this book.

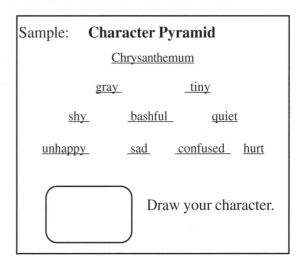

Sample: **Character Pyramid**

Chrysanthemum

gray   tiny

shy   bashful   quiet

unhappy   sad   confused   hurt

Draw your character.

Students can also fill out the maps about themselves.

Character Pyramid

Line 1   Name of character
Line 2   Two words describing physical appearance
Line 3   Three words describing personality
Line 4   Four words describing how this character feels at a certain point in the book

_____

_____ _____

_____ _____ _____

_____ _____ _____ _____

Draw your character.

Character Development

EMERGENT

DEVELOPING

➜ **INDEPENDENT**

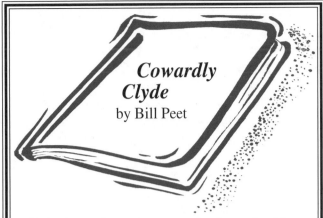

Cowardly Clyde
by Bill Peet

Clyde the warhorse is a coward at heart, but his master, Sir Galavant, is the bravest knight in the kingdom. They go off into the countryside to slay an ogre.

Activities

Have students brainstorm some words to describe Clyde: scared, determined, proud. Now have them prove it by verifying their opinions with specific things that happened in the story. For example:

skittish:	scarecrow gave him the creeps
coward:	hoped they wouldn't find the ogre
proud:	didn't want anyone to know he was a coward, pretended he was brave
determined:	galloped away, determined to save their necks
loyal:	went back to find his master

Talk about the changes that Clyde goes through.

Have students brainstorm what might have happened if Clyde was brave and Sir Galavant was a coward.

Literature Extensions

Have students write about a time when they felt scared. What happened or what did they do to overcome that fear? Do they still have that fear?

The character maps on pages 46 and 47 can be used as extensions with this book. When filling in the "Prove it" boxes on page 47, students can refer to the page number in the book where something happened instead of writing it out.

Sample: **Character Diamond**

Name:_____ Diamond:Character diamond

Title: Cowardly Clyde Author: Bill Peet

Clyde

horse brown

shy coward skittish

peace harmony left alone

coward scared determined loyal brave

fear ogre woods dogs

confident brave assured

proud supportive

Clyde

Character Diamond

Line 1   Name of character
Line 2   Two words describing physical appearance
Line 3   Three words describing personality
Line 4   Four words describing what the character wants
Line 5   Five words describing how the character develops
Line 6   Four words stating obstacles to be overcome
Line 7   Three words describing how the character feels
Line 8   Two words describing how you feel about the character
Line 9   Name of character

Name:_____ Diamond: _____

Title: _____ Author:_____

_____

_____ _____

_____ _____ _____

_____ _____ _____ _____

_____ _____ _____ _____ _____

_____ _____ _____ _____

_____ _____ _____

_____ _____

_____

Character Map

Name: _____

Title: _____

Author: _____

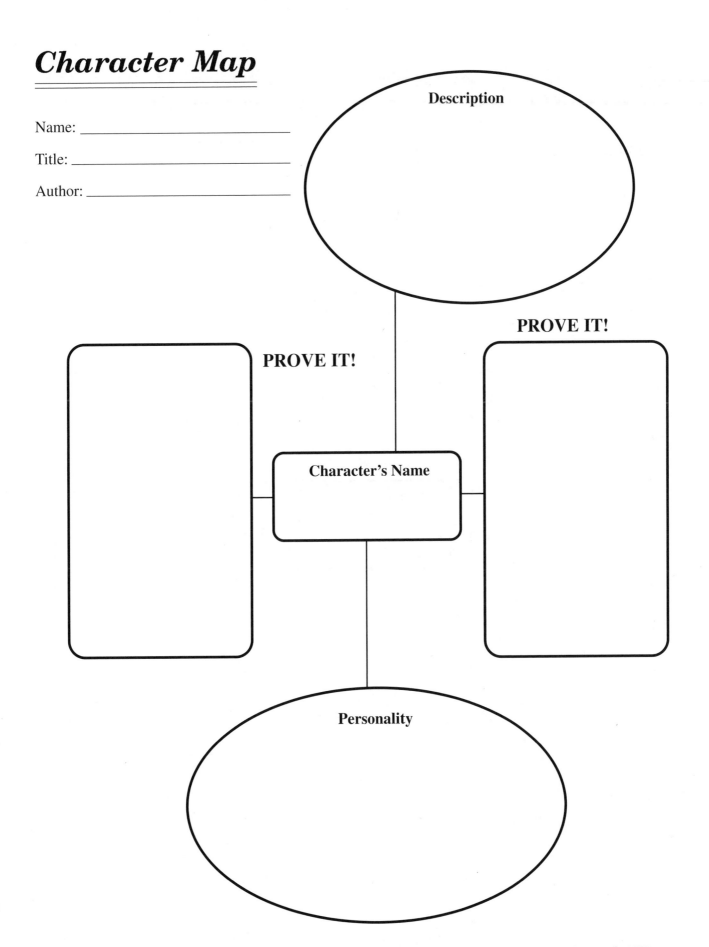

Description

PROVE IT!

PROVE IT!

Character's Name

Personality

Sample:

Character Map

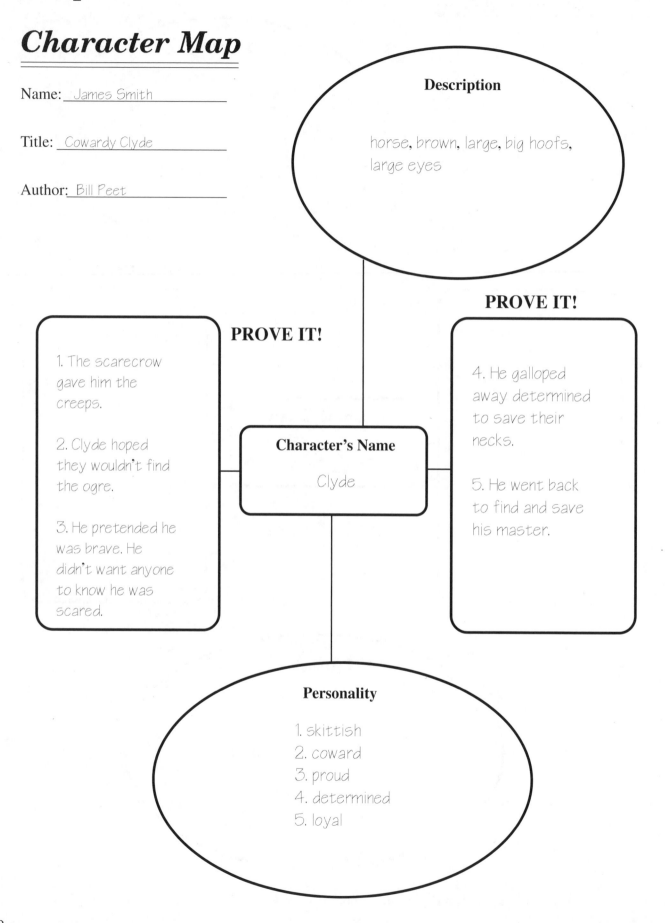

Name: James Smith

Title: Cowardy Clyde

Author: Bill Peet

Description

horse, brown, large, big hoofs, large eyes

PROVE IT!

1. The scarecrow gave him the creeps.

2. Clyde hoped they wouldn't find the ogre.

3. He pretended he was brave. He didn't want anyone to know he was scared.

Character's Name

Clyde

PROVE IT!

4. He galloped away determined to save their necks.

5. He went back to find and save his master.

Personality

1. skittish
2. coward
3. proud
4. determined
5. loyal

Color Words

→ **EMERGENT**
  DEVELOPING
  INDEPENDENT

Of Colors and Things
by Tana Hoban

This is a wordless book about colors. Each page is divided into four sections with a single object in each section. Each page represents a different color.

Activities

Unstaple this book and take it apart to laminate. Now you can write on each page and wipe off the text when you are done.

Go through the book with students and label each picture. You can write directly on each page or tape on a piece of paper.

Brainstorm with students all the objects around the room that are certain colors. Make a chart. For example:

RED flag thermos shirts	YELLOW chairs lunchbox paper
GREEN frogs books	

Literature Extensions

Make a class big book. Use large pieces of construction paper and glue colored ribbon on each page the same way the book has done. Using the interactive chart, students match the color words to objects of the corresponding color.

Each student can be responsible for one page or four students can work together on each page.

Students can also make their own books.

Color Words

EMERGENT
➡ **DEVELOPING**
INDEPENDENT

Who Said Red?
by Mary Serfozo

This book has a repetitive text. Each page gives many examples of things that are certain colors.

Sight Vocabulary

red	yellow	blue	green
purple	black	did	you
say	no	I	said

Activities

Using the interactive chart, students match the color words to objects that are that color.

You can have the objects already written on sentence strips or brainstorm and write them with students.

Students can make their own color books. Each color can have a two-page format.

red	fire engine
blue	sky
yellow	sunflower
green	grass
black	bat
purple	lilacs

Literature Extensions

Students can make their own color books. Each color can have a two-page format.

Page 1:

These things are always _____

Page 2

These things can be _____.

For example:

These things are always green:
grass
trees
stems
leaves
limes

These things can be green:
lollipops
notebooks
carpets
books

Color Words

EMERGENT
→ **DEVELOPING**
INDEPENDENT

Sight Vocabulary

red	yellow	blue
green	black	orange
car		

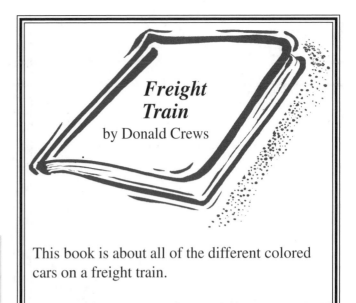

Freight Train by Donald Crews

This book is about all of the different colored cars on a freight train.

Activities

Make a train out of half-gallon milk or juice containers. Cut off one side of each container so it is open. Cover with construction paper and add wheels.

Have students fill the train with pictures of things that correspond to the color of each car.

You can also do this activity with large boxes or milk crates. Because the crates or boxes are so large, students can put actual items in them.

Literature Extensions

Students can make their own freight trains out of their snack and lunch milk cartons. Have them cover their milk cartons with construction paper and put in pictures of items that correspond to the cars' colors.

 Other suggested resources:

Beside the Bay by Sheila White Samton
Planting a Rainbow by Lois Ehlery
Mary Wore Her Red Dress by Merle Peek
Rain by Robert Kalan

Compare
and Contrast

→ **EMERGENT**
   DEVELOPING
   INDEPENDENT

Deep in the Forest
by Brinton Turkle

This wordless book follows the same format as *Goldilocks and the Three Bears* except three people live in the house and a little bear comes to visit while the people go out for a walk.

Activities

Compare and contrast *Deep in the Forest* and *Goldilocks and the Three Bears* using a Venn diagram drawn on a piece of chart or mural paper.

I rip apart and laminate all my wordless books. It's hard to do the first time, but it does get easier! Staple books back together with a long necked stapler. Books that were bound with glue can be put back together with spiral bindings, rings, or pipe cleaners. Students love writing on the actual pages of the book. Use overhead marking pens so pages can be wiped off.

Have students make up their own text to *Deep in the Woods*.

We write the text together. I use large chart paper so I can model the reading/writing process. We do one to five pages a day, depending on the attention span of my students. I then type the text and tape it on each page in the book. Because the book is laminated, the tape does not destroy it.

Literature
Extensions

Students can create their own same and different books.

Make a page that looks like this:

Deep in the Forest	Goldilocks

If students are making a "different" book, they can draw a picture of something that was different in each of the stories.

If students are making a "same" book, they can draw a picture of something that was the same in each of the stories.

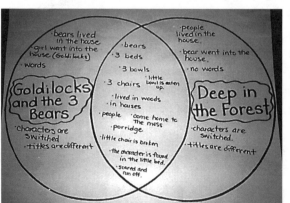

Students can do as many pages as they would like and then staple them together.

Compare
and Contrast

EMERGENT

➜ **DEVELOPING**

INDEPENDENT

The Three Javelinas
by Susan Lowell

This story is a Southwest version of *The Three Little Pigs* with javelinas instead of pigs. The story follows the same plot as the original.

Activities

Make a chart comparing this version of *The Three Little Pigs* with the original.

Three Javelinas	Three Pigs	Both Stories
javelinas	pigs	three of each
coyote	wolf	after three huffs and puffs to blow house down
first house tumbleweed	first house straw	first house not strong
second house sticks from cactus plant	second house sticks	second house not strong
third house adobe bricks	third house bricks	third house strong/solid
stove pipe	chimney	gets burned

Literature Extensions

Students make their own compare-and-contrast charts using the following versions of *The Three Little Pigs*:

The True Story of the Three Pigs
by Jon Scieszka

My Little Pigs
by David Bouchard

The Fourth Little Pig
by Teresa Celsi

Compare and Contrast

EMERGENT

DEVELOPING

➡ **INDEPENDENT**

Princess Furball
by Anita Lobel

Yeh-Shen by Ai-Ling Louie

Mufaro's Beautiful Daughters
by John Steptoe

The Egyptian Cinderella
by Shirley Climo

Cinderella by Charles Perrault

The Rough-Face Girl by Rafe Martin

These are all different versions of *Cinderella*.

Activities

Make a mural or a chart that lists titles of the *Cinderella* books and the following:

characters	language
setting	problem
illustrations	resolution

Talk about each of the categories listed above. Choose a book and fill in the chart together. Help students analyze the different elements. For example, when looking at the illustration category, my students said the pictures in *The Egyptian Cinderella* were crisp, clear, and had definite lines, while the illustrations from *Yeh-Shen* were blurry, not crisp and clear, and dreamy-like.

You can also use mural paper instead of poster board so the chart is much larger.

Literature Extensions

Have students pick any two things to compare and contrast using the Venn diagram on page 55. Students can choose:

two characters from same story (two sisters, Cinderella and a sister)
two characters from different stories
two settings from different books
two resolutions from different books, etc.

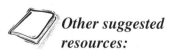***Other suggested resources:***

Little Red Riding Hood
Lon Po Po by Ed Young

Comprehension of Cumulative Stories

(where events are repeated and added to)

➡ **EMERGENT**

DEVELOPING

INDEPENDENT

Sight Vocabulary

jump	frog	the
that	water	

Jump, Frog, Jump
by Robert Kalan

Jump, Frog, Jump is about a frog who gets away from trouble by jumping away.

Activities

Act out the story using headband masks. Have students make pictures of the different characters:

> a fly
> turtle
> frog
> net
> fish
> three different hats
> snake

Put the pictures onto a strip of paper to make headband masks.

Talk about characteristics of cumulative tales.

Literature Extensions

Students can write their own class story. Have them choose an animal and decide how the animal will get away. For example, a kangaroo or rabbit can jump, a snake can slither, a dog can run, etc. Using the same format as *Jump, Frog, Jump*, students can make their own version.

 Other suggested resource:

Who Sank the Boat? by Pamela Allen

Comprehension of Cumulative Stories

(where events are repeated and added to)

EMERGENT
→ **DEVELOPING**
INDEPENDENT

The Napping House
by Audrey Wood

The Napping House is a story about what is happening in a house during the evening when everyone is sleeping. That is, until a flea bites the mouse . . .

Sight Vocabulary

house	napping
sleeping	on
who	the

Activities

Have some students make a picture of a bed on a piece of poster board or chart paper. Other students can make the characters in the story: granny, boy, dog, cat, and mouse. Use a kidney bean as the flea. Use the pictures to retell the story.

Talk about cause and effect. Students can act out the causes and effects and do some chanting in between.

For example:

> The flea bit the mouse.
> CHANT "Then what happened?"
> They scared the cat.
> CHANT "Then what happened?"
> The cat clawed the dog.
> CHANT "Then what happened?"

Literature Extensions

Talk about how each character in the story is introduced and then described.

. . . there is a granny, a snoring granny.
. . . there is a child, a dreaming child.

How else can the characters be described?

Students can make their own paper bag storyboards (see page 9).

Students could also use a small paper lunch bag as the bed. Stuff it with newspaper or paper towels so it becomes 3-D.

Comprehension of Cumulative Stories

(where events are repeated and added to)

EMERGENT

DEVELOPING

➔ **INDEPENDENT**

Sight Vocabulary

picture	book	wrote
that	this	

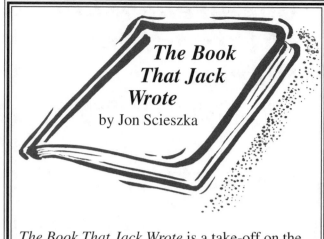

The Book That Jack Wrote

by Jon Scieszka

The Book That Jack Wrote is a take-off on the story *The House That Jack Built.*

Activities

Write the repetitive phrases on sentence strips. Using the interactive chart, students can sequence events and also match the cause with the effect.

That flung the pie flying through the air,

That beaned the baby humming the tune,

That tossed the cow sailing over the moon,

That spooked the dog,

That chased the cat,

That ate the rat . . .

 Other suggested resource:

The House That Jack Built, illustrated by Jenny Stow

Literature Extensions

Students each create their own book titled:

The Book That (child's name) *Wrote*

or

Each student could add a page to a class book titled:

The Book That (class name) *Wrote*

Contractions: n't, 've, 's

EMERGENT
➡ **DEVELOPING**
INDEPENDENT

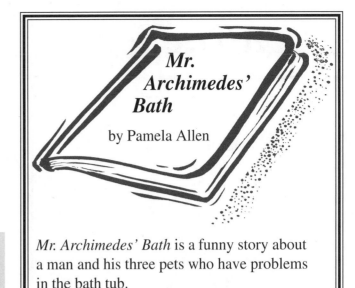

Mr. Archimedes' Bath is a funny story about a man and his three pets who have problems in the bath tub.

Activities

Talk about contractions. What are they? How are they formed? What do they mean? Then find the following contractions in the story:

> it's
> don't
> didn't
> where's
> let's
> wasn't
> I've
> that's

Graph the contractions according to their patterns.

not	is	have	us
do not	it is		
did not	where is		let us
was not	that is	I have	

Have students add more contractions to each category.

Literature Extensions

Students can pretend they are one of the animals. Have them write what they would say to Mr. Archimedes. What would they say before he figured out the problem? What would they say after? Students need to use contractions in their responses.

Do some science experiments with displacement. Students can work individually or in pairs. Give each student a bucket of water and some objects that can get wet. How many objects can be put into the bucket before the water overflows? Have students write predictions and then respond to the actual results.

Students could make lines in the bucket about a half-inch apart. Then they can predict how far the water will rise as each new object is added. They should use contractions in their predictions:

> I think it's going to rise to the second line.

> The water isn't going to overflow when I add this tile.

Contraction 'll

EMERGENT
➔ **DEVELOPING**
INDEPENDENT

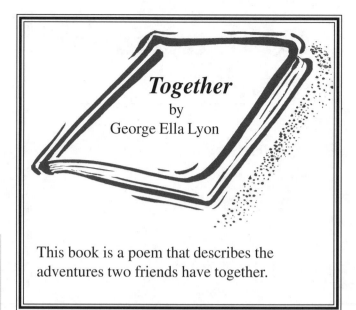

Together
by
George Ella Lyon

This book is a poem that describes the adventures two friends have together.

Activities

This poem is a dialogue between two friends. It follows the repetitive pattern of "if you'll do this, then I'll do this." The contractions **I'll** and **you'll** are found on almost every page.

Talk about making contractions with the word will. Brainstorm all of the words that can be made:

> I'll
> she'll
> he'll
> we'll
> they'll
> you'll

These can be added under a "will" heading on the chart explained on page 59.

The contraction **let's** is also found in the refrain: "Let's put our heads together and dream the same dream." Talk about what two words form this contraction.

Literature Extensions

Students can pair up and make their own books using the same predictable pattern found in *Together*. First have them brainstorm all of the things they could do together. After they have a list of activities/adventures, they can think of what I'll do and what you'll do.

Instead of having students make their own books, all of the pages can be put together into a class big book.

Students could each make a page writing and illustrating what "I'll do." Next, put all of these pages upside down on the floor and have students pick one. They now have to add the second part of the page that tells what "you'll do."

Contractions:
(Many Different Kinds)

EMERGENT
DEVELOPING
➜ **INDEPENDENT**

Hubert's Hair-Raising Adventure
by Bill Peet

This story is about a lion named Hubert who is very vain. A spark flies onto his mane, and he loses all of his hair. His friends try to help him solve this problem.

Activities

This book is loaded with contractions. After students read the story, have them go back and find all of the contractions. Make a list.

isn't	I'm	what'll
I'd	you're	I've
it's	I'll	won't
we're	he'd	you've
he'll	there's	that's
don't	wasn't	they'll
aren't	that's	they'd
you'd	didn't	she'd
we've	you'll	there'll

After generating the above list, students can categorize them in different ways. For example, they can categorize them by what has been replaced by the apostrophe:

they'd, she'd, you'd, I'd, he'd

They can also categorize them by the first word. For example:

I'm, I'd, I've, I'll

Literature Extensions

Hubert was very vain about his hair. Have students think about the other animals in the story. What might they have been vain about and what could have happened to embarrass them? For example:

The hyena came down with laryngitis and lost his laugh.

The crocodile lost his teeth.

Students should use contractions in their stories.

Other Bill Peet books that are good models for contractions are:
Cyrus the Unsinkable Sea Serpent
Smokey
Huge Harold
How Droofus the Dragon Lost His Head

Days of the Week

→ **EMERGENT**
   DEVELOPING
   INDEPENDENT

Seven Eggs

by Meredith Hooper

This is a story about seven eggs that hatch, one on each day of the week.

Sight Vocabulary

on	the	out
a	came	cracked
and	egg	

Activities

Make a chart of the story using the repetitive text.

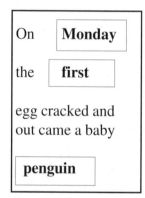

On [**Monday**]

the [**first**]

egg cracked and out came a baby

[**penguin**]

Make a slit in the poster board and slip in a paper clip to hold the cards.

Literature Extensions

Brainstorm with students all of the things that hatch from eggs. Ruth Heller's book *Chickens Aren't the Only Ones* is an excellent resource to read aloud to children.

Have students make their own books in the shape of an egg. On each page they need to write the day of the week and what hatched out of the egg. Use the pattern below for the pages and then bind the books together with rubber bands.

Pattern:

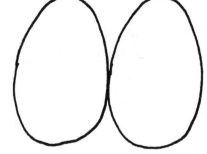

Give each student five pages for his/her book. Open the book to the middle page and put a rubber band around it.

Activity

Make some sandwich boards for students to wear.

Seven students can wear the sandwich boards while others put them in order.

Days of the Week

EMERGENT
➡ **DEVELOPING**
INDEPENDENT

Cookie's Week
by Cindy Ward

Cookie's Week is a story about a cat named Cookie and all the mischief she gets into every day.

Sight Vocabulary

on	there	was
everywhere	the	Sunday
Monday	Tuesday	Wednesday
Thursday	Friday	Saturday

Activities

Make cards for each day of the week. Have students put them in order.

After the cards are in order, have students brainstorm the specials they have each day: art, music, gym, library, computer, etc. Match the specials to the days of the week.

Literature Extensions

Rewrite *Cookie's Week* with Cookie having different adventures every day. Depending on your class size, your book might be titled *Cookie's Month*.

Students can be given a paper with the story line already there, or they can write their own.

Students can write their own book about a pet they have or would like to have. How might their pet get in trouble?

This could also be done as a class book. Each page would be done by a different child about his/her pet.

 Other suggested resources:

Peep's Diary by John Astrop
Boss for a Week by Libby Handy
Today Is Monday by Eric Carle
The New Kid on the Block by Jack Prelutsky ("Suzanna Socked Me Sunday," page 121)

NAME Christopher Chiappa.

On SUNDAY........

Cookie Jamtupinto the rof

There was/were shngul
everywhere!

NAME Chris G.

On SUNDAY........

Cookie Gat in to the refagrt

There was/were fod
everywhere!

NAME Melissa

On SUNDAY........

Cookie chalyst the GRBiG TRUK

There was/were GRBiG
everywhere!

Days of the Week

EMERGENT
➡ **DEVELOPING**
INDEPENDENT

Sight Vocabulary

Monday	Tuesday	Wednesday
Thursday	Friday	Saturday
Sunday	through	still
hungry	he	one

The Very Hungry Caterpillar
by Eric Carle

This story is about a caterpillar who eats his way through the days of the week before turning into a butterfly.

Activities

Make cards for each day of the week. Have students match the day of the week to the food the caterpillar ate.

Monday

Tuesday

Wednesday

Make pictures of the foods the hungry caterpillar ate through. Cut out a hole in the middle of each food. Use a sock or a "draft dodger" for the caterpillar. As students retell the story, they can eat through the foods.

Literature Extensions

Students can make their own *Hungry Caterpillar* books by picking different foods the caterpillar could eat during the week.

Have students choose an animal they are interested in. They can make animal-shape books where their animal eats through the week, but whatever the animal eats must be something it really could eat.

Drawing Conclusions

➡ **EMERGENT**
DEVELOPING
INDEPENDENT

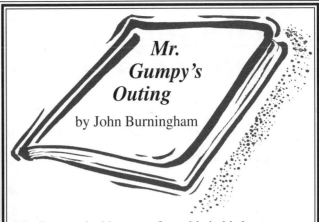

Mr. Gumpy's Outing

by John Burningham

Mr. Gumpy decides to go for a ride in his boat. Many children and animals ask if they can go along. He gives them permission, but only if they "behave." Problems arise once they are all in the boat.

Activities

Ask students to draw conclusions about why Mr. Gumpy tells the children and animals they mustn't do certain things if they want to go with him.

Make cards for the animals and what they were not supposed to do. Make the following chart to clip cards on.

sheep	bleat

pig	muck about

chickens	flap around

Mr. Gumpy told the rabbit

please do not

hop about.

WHY?

Literature Extensions

Make a class big book. Have each student draw a picture of another animal that could have gone with Mr. Gumpy. What advice would Mr. Gumpy give the animal? For example:

horse	do not whinny
mosquito	do not bite
cow	do not moo
bird	do not flap your feathers

Drawing Conclusions

EMERGENT
→ **DEVELOPING**
INDEPENDENT

The Mitten
by Jan Brett

Nicki drops his new mitten in the snow. Different animals find the mitten and want to use it as a home.

Activities

There are many conclusions and inferences students can make after listening to or reading this story. Use a box and arrow design to show students how you can make inferences and conclusions when given some information.

Baba didn't want to knit white mittens.	Why? →	Couldn't be found in the snow if dropped.
Mole moved over when he saw rabbit's big kickers.	Why? →	Rabbit could hurt him.
They didn't argue with the hedgehog.	Why? →	Hedgehog had prickles and could stick them.
They all quickly let owl in.	Why? →	They could get hurt by owl's glinty talons.

Literature Extensions

Have students make a class book called *Draw Your Own Conclusions*. Make it in the shape of a mitten.

Who else could have wanted to move into the mitten? How would the animals already in the mitten respond to the new intruder? For example:

Front page

A skunk wanted to move in.

All the animals moved over!

Back page

Nobody wanted him to spray them.

Drawing Conclusions

EMERGENT

DEVELOPING

➜ **INDEPENDENT**

Cam Jansen and the Mystery of the Dinosaur Bones
by David Adler

This mystery is about a museum that has some missing dinosaur bones. Cam's photographic memory helps solve the puzzle.

Activities

Cam Jansen books are excellent resources for demonstrating the skill of drawing conclusions. In this book, Cam constantly draws conclusions based on things she sees.

Conclusions	Evidence the conclusions were based upon.
The teacher wants us to be quiet.	Teacher stood on a chair with a finger over her mouth.
The bones can't be taken when the museum is open.	Too many people and guards around. Would take too long to unhook a bone.
Cam knew the milkman was picking up something else.	Milk is not delivered in the late afternoon. The museum used a different company.
Cam thought they succeeded in hiding in the museum.	People walked past the case. Everything got quiet.

Literature Extensions

Students can read other Cam Jansen books and make some conclusion and evidence boxes similar to the activity.

Some other Cam Jansen books include:
Cam Jansen and the . . .
Mystery of the U.F.O.
Mystery of the Television Dog
Mystery of the Gold Coin
Mystery of the Circus Clown
Mystery of the Stolen Corn Popper

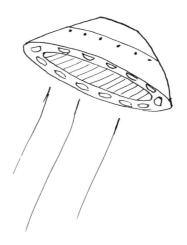

Main Idea and Supporting Details

→ **EMERGENT**
DEVELOPING
INDEPENDENT

More Spaghetti I Say
by Rita Golden Gelman

Minnie is a monkey who loves spaghetti. She doesn't have time to play with her friend because she is so busy eating and playing with her spaghetti.

Sight Vocabulary

I	love
can	and
spaghetti	in

Activities

The main idea of this story is that Minnie loves spaghetti so much she doesn't have time to play with her friend Freddy. She eats too much and then is ready to play, but now Freddy starts to like the spaghetti. Talk about this with students, and then talk about the details.

How did she eat the spaghetti?
   . . . with pancakes, ice cream and ham, pickles and cookies, bananas and jam, mustard and marshmallow stuff, etc.

What can she do with spaghetti?
   . . . run in it, ride in it, jump, slide, hide, skate, and ski on it, etc.

 Other suggested resource:

Why Can't I Fly? by Rita Golden Gelman

Literature Extensions

Students can make a spaghetti big book. Give each student some yellow yarn. Have them pretend the yellow yarn is spaghetti and put it into a picture.

What else can Minnie do with spaghetti?

Students can use themselves as the character instead of Minnie. What would they like to do with spaghetti?

Main Idea and Supporting Details

EMERGENT
→ **DEVELOPING**
INDEPENDENT

Cluck One
by Louise Matthews

This is a story about a weasel that decides he will play a number of tricks on a hen who has just laid an egg. But in the end, the joke is on him.

Activities

Brainstorm with students the main idea and supporting details of this story.

The main idea is that weasel sees the cuckoo play a trick on the hen. He is now playing the same trick a number of times on the hen by putting different kinds of eggs in her nest. In the end, he is the one who ends up getting fooled.

Now talk about the details.

Cuckoo puts in a blue egg.
Weasel puts in:
    a green egg found by the marsh,
    a shiny egg found by a hedge,
    an ostrich egg, and
    an egg found in the sand by the ocean.

When we start to talk about the main idea, I ask students to tell me what they think and I write it on the board. After we have brainstormed, we look at our list. We go over each point and decide whether it is a supporting detail or the main idea. We begin to erase the supporting ideas until we have only the main idea left.

Instead of erasing, we sometimes circle the supporting details.

Literature Extensions

What other kinds of eggs could the weasel have found and put in the hen's nest? Students can write new details about weasel finding the other eggs and what would happen when they grew up.

For example:

a snake egg would hiss in the sun

a frilled lizard would screech all day

an owl would hoot all night

Main Idea and Supporting Details

EMERGENT

DEVELOPING

➜ **INDEPENDENT**

Flat Stanley by Jeff Brown

This story is about a boy who wakes up in the morning to find himself as flat as a pancake. He has many adventures that are funny, scary, and exciting.

Activities

Talk about the difference between a main idea and a supporting detail.

Identify both of these in the story *Flat Stanley.*

Main Idea:

Stanley becomes as flat as a pancake and has many adventures because of his new size. He eventually becomes normal size again.

Supporting Details:
how he becomes flat
all of his adventures
how he becomes himself again

Literature Extensions

Have students think about what other adventures Stanley could have. What places could he go? What could he do? Students can make individual books or put all of the adventures together in a class book.

What would happen if the main idea of the story changed?
What if:
Stanley became as small as a flea?
Stanley grew as tall as a giant?
Stanley blew up like a balloon?

How does changing the main idea change the supporting details? What details still could have happened? Which ones could not have happened?

Other suggested resources:

The Emperor's New Clothes
Chester the Worldly Pig by Bill Peet

Name Recognition

→ **EMERGENT**

DEVELOPING

INDEPENDENT

Sight Vocabulary

wore	her
his	all
day	long

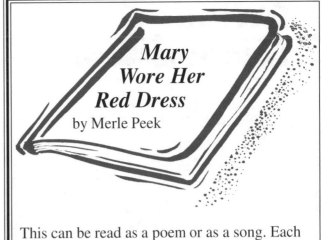

Mary Wore Her Red Dress by Merle Peek

This can be read as a poem or as a song. Each verse names a child and tells what s/he is wearing all day long.

Activities

Write children's names and what they are wearing on separate strips of paper. Using the interactive chart, place all the clothing strips on the right side of the chart. Place all of the name strips on the floor.

Say, "I spy someone who is wearing a yellow dress." That child would find her name strip on the floor and put it next to the yellow dress strip.

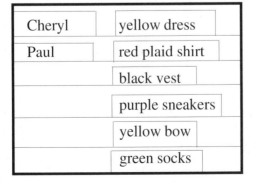

Cheryl	yellow dress
Paul	red plaid shirt
	black vest
	purple sneakers
	yellow bow
	green socks

Literature Extensions

Create your own class song.
Make a master page that looks like this:

* _____	
wore _____	
* _____	
wore _____ all day long.	

Have students draw pictures of what they are wearing. Give children this master to write in their names where the stars are. Depending on your students' abilities, you can write in the rest, or they can use invented spelling. Put all of the pages together and sing.

Name Recognition

→ **EMERGENT**

DEVELOPING

INDEPENDENT

"Whose Birthday Is It?"
from *Butterscotch Dreams*
by Sonja Dunn

Sight Vocabulary

birthday   party
is   here

Activities

Write the poem on a chart using your students' names.

Whose birthday is it?

Is (student's name) here?
Uh Huh
Is (student's name) here?
Uh Huh
Is (student's name) here?
Uh Huh

 Other suggested resources:

Brown Bear Brown Bear, What Do You See? by Bill Martin Jr.
Polar Bear Polar Bear, What Do You Hear? by Bill Martin Jr.
(Students can put their names in place of the animals' names.)

Literature Extensions

Students can draw pictures of themselves to put next to their names on the chart.

Have students think about a birthday party. What kinds of things would be at a party? What games would be played? What foods would be served? Students can each make their own *Birthday Party Book* and label all of the things that they would have, eat, and do at the party.

Balloons, Cake
and Presents

Number Words

The Balancing Act: A Counting Book
by Merle Peek

This poem/song has a repetitive text. One elephant is balancing on a piece of string. He invites a friend, and then two elephants are on the string. They invite a friend; three elephants are on the string, etc.

➡ **EMERGENT**
DEVELOPING
INDEPENDENT

Sight Vocabulary

step   on
a   elephant

Activities

Go to the gym and use a balance beam to act out this poem/song. We lowered the balance beam so it was only a foot off the floor.

Have students make large pictures of elephants with long trunks. Tie a piece of string or yarn between two chairs and have students hang their elephants up by the trunk. Use these props to act out the poem/song.

Make number word cards and have students match the correct number of elephants to each number word.

Literature Extensions

Make a class book. Lay the number cards out on the floor and have students each take a card. They need to draw the corresponding number of animals balancing on a string. Put all of the pages together in order. If you have a large class, you might have two or three books going from one to ten.

Think about other things elephants could balance on. Students make their own counting book of an animal balancing on something.

For example:

bears on tires
ants on a log
lions on balls

 Other suggested resources:

Animal Sleepyheads 1 to 10 by Joanna Cole
Five Little Monkeys Jumping on the Bed
    by Eileen Christelow
How Many Bugs in a Box? by David A.
    Carter

Number Words

EMERGENT
➜ **DEVELOPING**
INDEPENDENT

Who Wants One?

by Mary Serfozo

A little girl with a magician's box conjures up all kinds of surprises for her brother. She gives him things in groups of two, three, etc. The number words appear from five to seven times on each page.

Sight Vocabulary

one	two	three	four
five	six	seven	eight
nine	ten	do	you

Activities

Play Concentration. Have ten students stand up in front of the room. Each child will have a card with a picture of so many items (one, two, three items, etc.).

Children hold their cards with the pictures facing them.

Pass cards with number words on them to students who are sitting. A student with a number card will ask a child in front of the room to turn his/her card around. If it is a match, the "number word" will sit on the floor in front of the picture with the matching number of items.

Literature Extensions

Students can make their own books using the same repetitive format as *Who Wants One?* Keep the same two beginning lines of each page and the same last line. Students can create their own text in between.

> Do you pick six?
> Look, here is six.

Six_____, six_____, six_____
six_____

Do you want (the number word)?

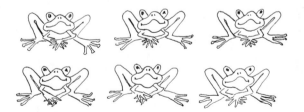

Point of View: First Person

EMERGENT

DEVELOPING

➜ **INDEPENDENT**

The True Story of the Three Pigs

by Jon Scieszka

This book is a retelling of *The Three Little Pigs* through the eyes of the wolf.

Activities

Talk about the differences between stories written in the first and third person. Brainstorm with students the signals that tell this book is written in the first person.

Compare and contrast each event that happened in the wolf's version and the original story of *The Three Little Pigs* (**TTLP**). For example:

Wolf: I went over to ask for a cup of sugar.

TTLP: The wolf went over to eat the pigs.

Wolf: I didn't huff and puff and blow the straw house down; I sneezed!

TTLP: The wolf deliberately blew down the house.

The original versions of *The Three Little Pigs* are mostly done in third person. Have students brainstorm some of the things that might be said if this were told in the first person from one of the pig's point of view.

Literature Extensions

Rewrite the book from one of the pig's point of view.

Choose another book and write it from a first person point of view. Some books that my students have chosen to do this activity with are:

   Three Billy Goats Gruff from the Troll's point of view

   Hansel and Gretel from the witch's point of view

   Little Red Riding Hood from the wolf's point of view

   The Three Bears from Goldilocks' point of view

Point of View: Third Person

EMERGENT

DEVELOPING

→ **INDEPENDENT**

Caps for Sale

by Esphyr Slobodkina

This story is about a peddler who is selling caps. He sits down to take a nap and his caps disappear.

Activities

Talk about the differences between stories written in the first and third person. Brainstorm with students the signals that tell this book is written in the third person.

Have students take turns and read excerpts from other books they are reading. Decide whether they are written in the first or third person.

Talk about traditional tales such as:
> *The Three Little Pigs*
> *The Three Bears*
> *Three Billy Goats Gruff*
> *Little Red Riding Hood*
> *Hansel and Gretel*
> *Snow White and the Seven*
>   *Dwarfs*
> *The Gingerbread Boy*

How would these stories be different if told from one character's point of view (first person)?

Literature Extensions

Rewrite the story from the peddler's point of view.

Rewrite the story from the monkey's point of view.

Predicting

➡ **EMERGENT**

DEVELOPING

INDEPENDENT

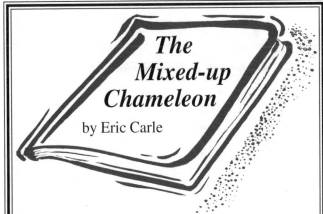

The Mixed-up Chameleon
by Eric Carle

This story is about a chameleon who wishes he could be like other animals in the zoo. He gets his wish and takes on some attributes from each one.

Sight Vocabulary

I	wish
could	be
like	a

Activities

Begin reading the book to students. After reading the page where the chameleon meets the polar bear, stop showing students the pictures. Have them predict what will happen after he wishes he could be like each animal.

As you read each page, have students take turns coming up to a piece of chart paper and drawing what the chameleon might look like after each wish. Then look at the pictures in the book and compare them with students' ideas.

Have students brainstorm the attributes of each animal that the chameleon meets and what changes could have happened:

> flamingo — beak, long neck
> fox — pointed ears, long snout
> fish — scales, gills, tail
> deer — tail, etc.

Literature Extensions

Students can make their own books about the chameleon meeting other animals. What might the chameleon wish for, and what attribute might he receive? Some examples include:

> I wish I could hop like a bunny — long ears, floppy ears, tail
> I wish I could roar like a lion — mane, tail
> I wish I could sing like a bird — feathers, wings, beak
> I wish I could buzz like a bee — wings, yellow stripes

Students can begin their stories with an animal other than a chameleon.

What if students made the wishes themselves? What would happen to them?

Predicting

EMERGENT
➜ **DEVELOPING**
INDEPENDENT

Why Can't I Fly?
by Rita Golden Gelman

This story is about a monkey named Minnie who wants to fly. She seeks the advice of her animal friends who can fly. Her friends tell her that in order to fly she must have a certain attribute that they have.

Sight Vocabulary

fly	goodbye	can
can't	climbed	

Activities

Brainstorm a list of all animals that can fly. Then predict what kind of advice each animal would give Minnie. For example, a butterfly would tell Minnie she had to have wings. A ladybug would tell Minnie she had to have spots.

Make a chart:

animal	advice
owl	say whoo whoo
eagle	paint your head white
bee	say bzzzzz or paint yourself yellow and black
bird	sing a song

Literature Extensions

Students can have Minnie try to learn to do something else and follow the same story line. Make up a chart that looks like this:

What will Minnie want to do?	
animal	**advice**

Students can use the chart as a brainstorming activity. They can work in pairs, groups, or individually. After writing down ideas, students can write a story.

This idea came from one of my students, Adam Belanger.

Minnie is trying to jump.

She met a frog.
"That's not how you
do it. You have to
paint yourself
green."

Predicting

EMERGENT

DEVELOPING

➜ **INDEPENDENT**

Q Is for Duck
by Mary Elting
and Michael Folsom

In this alphabet book, students need to predict what each letter stands for.

Activities

This is a very easy-to-read book for the independent reader, but it is an excellent catalyst for students to write their own predicting books based on science and social studies themes, as well as age-appropriate reading materials.

Have students predict what each letter stands for.

For example: D is for Mole . . . .

Possibilities include:
    because moles dig in the dirt
    because moles get dirty when they dig

What did students base their predictions on?

Literature Extensions

Make a class book following the same format as *Q is for Duck*. Each student can choose a letter of the alphabet and use a science or social studies theme. For example:

I is for rock
    because igneous is a kind of rock.

M is for rock
    because metamorphic is a kind of rock.

H is for scientific method
    because hypothesizing is a step in the scientific method.

Students can also use a piece of literature they are reading as the theme. For example:

R is for *James and the Giant Peach*
    because Roald Dahl is the author.

N is for Aunt Sponge and Aunt Spiker
    because they are nasty.

Students can share their book with another class. Have the audience try to guess what each letter represents.

Prepositions

EMERGENT
➡ **DEVELOPING**
INDEPENDENT

Rosie's Walk is about a hen who takes a walk through the farm and is followed by a fox.

Sight Vocabulary

the   for

Activities

Using props from the classroom, have students put themselves into different places: under the desk, over the chair, between the books, in front of the piano, etc.

Write the story on sentence strips. Using the interactive chart, students can put the story in order. Use highlighting tape to highlight all of the prepositions. (This tape is available from Crystal Springs Books, 1-800-321-0401.)

 Other suggested resources:

Over, Under and Through by Tana Hoban
Guinea Pigs Far and Near by Kate Duke

Literature Extensions

Think of other predator/prey relationships:

eagle — rabbit
leopard — zebra
snake — mouse
cat — bird

Have students brainstorm where the prey is going to go:

through the log
over the bush
around the tree, etc.

The prey could be unaware of its predator, like in *Rosie's Walk,* or it could be aware of its predator and is running away. Students can then put their ideas into a book, mural, or picture.

Prepositions

EMERGENT

DEVELOPING

➜ **INDEPENDENT**

Wheel Away! is about a wheel from a bicycle that gets away from a boy and travels all around the town: under the shirts, across the dirt, between the pens . . . .

Sight Vocabulary

through	down	over	under
across	goes	between	climbing
slowing			

Activities

List all of the prepositions from the story.

Think of other places the wheel could have gone and list them.

      in the barn

      through the hay

      over the rocks

Have each student choose a new place for the wheel to go and illustrate it on a strip of calculator or register tape. Put all of the strips together for a long class adventure.

Literature Extensions

Students can make their own wheel adventures. Have students think of something that could get away from them: baseball, frisbee, tire, yo-yo, etc. Students can make their own books following the same format as *Wheel Away*!

Make a class mural. Think of and illustrate other places the wheel could have gone. Students can work individually or in small groups.

Print Concepts

(see page 25 for a list of specific print concepts)

➡ **EMERGENT**
  DEVELOPING
  INDEPENDENT

It Looked Like Spilt Milk

by Charles Shaw

Each page in this book has a white shape on a blue background. The shapes could be spilt milk, but they aren't. They are clouds.

Sight Vocabulary

| sometimes | it | milk | but |
| looked | like | spilt | wasn't |

Activities

Point to each word as the book is read.

Point out the differences between letters, words, and sentences.

Chart the story leaving out the second line of each page. Write the second line of each page on sentence strips. Have students arrange the sentence strips on the interactive chart where they belong.

Literature Extensions

Take a small pitcher of water and add a little milk to it so it turns white. Pour some onto a table or tray and have students decide what it looks like.

Give students white paper for them to tear or cut into different shapes. Make your own *It Looks Like Spilt Milk* class book.

Go outside with clipboards on a cloudy day. Have students lie down and look at the clouds. Have them draw and label what they see.

| Sometimes it looked like Spilt Milk. |
| |
| Sometimes it looked like a Rabbit. |
| |
| Sometimes it looked like a Bird. |
| |

But it wasn't Spilt Milk.

But it wasn't a Rabbit.

But it wasn't a Bird.

Punctuation

→ **EMERGENT**
DEVELOPING
INDEPENDENT

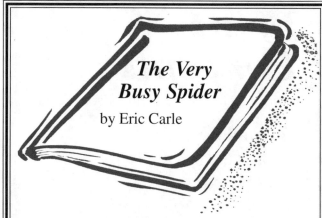

The Very Busy Spider
by Eric Carle

This is a repetitive, predictable book about a spider who is busy spinning a web. Many animals come to ask her to play with them, but she never answers them. She is too busy spinning her web.

Activities

This is an excellent book to use as an introduction to punctuation marks. Every other page has the following format:

"____! ____!" said the ____.
  ("Oink! Oink!" grunted the pig.)

"Want to _____?"
  ("want to roll in the mud?")

Point out each punctuation mark and discuss the following questions:

Why is the exclamation point after each noise the animal makes?

Why are there quotation marks around each sound and each question?

Why is the question mark there?

Literature Extensions

Brainstorm with students other animals that could have talked to the spider. Predict what they might have said and asked.

For example:
  "Quack! Quack!" said the duck.
  "Want to swim in the pond?"

  "Baa! Baa!" said the sheep.
  "Want to eat some grass?"

The animals in the story were mostly farm animals. Who would the spider have met if this took place at the zoo? Do the same activity as above, but use zoo animals.

For example:
  "Growl! Growl!" said the bear.
  "Want to eat some berries?"

  "Roar! Roar!" said the lion.
  "Want to lie in the sun?"

Each student can pick an animal and make one page for a class big book.

Punctuation

EMERGENT

➡ **DEVELOPING**

INDEPENDENT

Yo! Yes?

by Chris Raschka

This book is eight lines long and shows how punctuation affects the meaning of what you are reading.

Activities

Discuss how the meaning of something that is said changes when different punctuation is used.

For example:

Hello?

Hello!

Hello.

Oh?

Oh!

Oh.

Oh . . .

Literature Extensions

Have students draw pictures of the same word and how its meaning changes based on the punctuation used.

or

Have students write a sentence that would explain the meaning of the punctuation.
For example:

I just hit a home run.
Mom!

I need to get this note signed that tells why I had to go to the principal's office.
Mom . . .

I wonder what's for dinner?
Mom.

I hear a noise. I'm worried.
Mom?

Punctuation
(Quotation Marks)

EMERGENT
➡ **DEVELOPING**
INDEPENDENT

Sight Vocabulary

said	Grandma	cookies	rang
nobody	doorbell	smell	share

The
Doorbell
Rang
by Pat Hutchins

The Doorbell Rang is a story about a plate of cookies that needs to be shared among friends. Every time the doorbell rings more children come in and the cookies must be split accordingly.

Activities

Make some sandwich board quotation marks and commas for students to wear.

Write some statements from the book on sentence strips. Have one student stand up and hold the statement. Have the students wearing the quotation marks and commas come up and put themselves where they should be. The statement strips will have to be cut. Students love doing that.

 Come in said Ma.

 Come in said Ma.

Literature Extensions

Have students make some word problems about having to share cookies. For example:

I had four cookies. I gave one cookie to my friend Rich to eat at snack time. How many cookies did I get to eat?

$$4-1=3$$

Put all of the word problems together into a book. Make a copy for each student to have and do.

Have students think about what other things each person in the story might have said every time the doorbell rang. One student can talk into a tape recorder and another child can write out the conversation and put in the quotation marks. Students enjoy talking into the tape recorder and listening to each other.

Punctuation
(Quotation Marks)

EMERGENT
→ **DEVELOPING**
INDEPENDENT

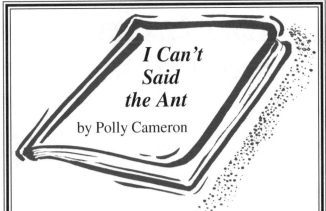

*I Can't
Said
the Ant*

by Polly Cameron

This book is about a teapot who fell onto the floor. All of the kitchen products come to her rescue and try to get her back up on the stove. It is filled with rhyme and conversation.

Activities

Write down some of the statements the kitchen utensils make. Do not put quotation marks around them. Color some dry elbow macaroni in a mixture of alcohol and food coloring. Have students come up and glue on the elbow macaroni where the quotation marks and commas belong.

| What's all the clatter asked the platter? |

| Pick her up said the cup. |

| Teapot fell said the dinner bell. |

Literature Extensions

Have students come up with other items in the kitchen and write their own rhymes with quotation marks.

Take the word "said" and try to put in another word. Make an "Instead of Said" chart. For example:

Instead of Said	
yelled	asked
whispered	shouted
mumbled	complained
shrieked	joked
whimpered	gasped
exclaimed	declared

 Other suggested resource:

Sing a Song of Popcorn, Selected Poems,
edited by Beatrice Schenk DeRegniers
("Five Little Squirrels," page 10)

Punctuation
(Quotation Marks)

EMERGENT

DEVELOPING

→ **INDEPENDENT**

Frog and Toad books are about a frog and a toad who are friends and have many adventures together.

Activities

Almost every page of *Frog and Toad* books is filled with quotation marks. Point out the quotation marks as you talk about the story.

Use the sentence strips students made for literature extensions to do an activity with the interactive chart. Make some strips shown below:

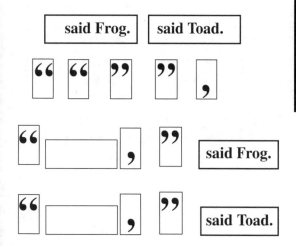

Put students' dialogue strips on the interactive chart. Then put in the quotation marks, commas, and who said it.

Literature Extensions

Students can write their own *Frog and Toad* adventures that include conversations. (See sample on next page.)

Have students make up dialogue between Frog and Toad and put them on sentence strips to be used during an activity time.

Generate an "Instead of Said" chart (see page 89). After writing stories, students use the chart and change all the saids to more descriptive words.

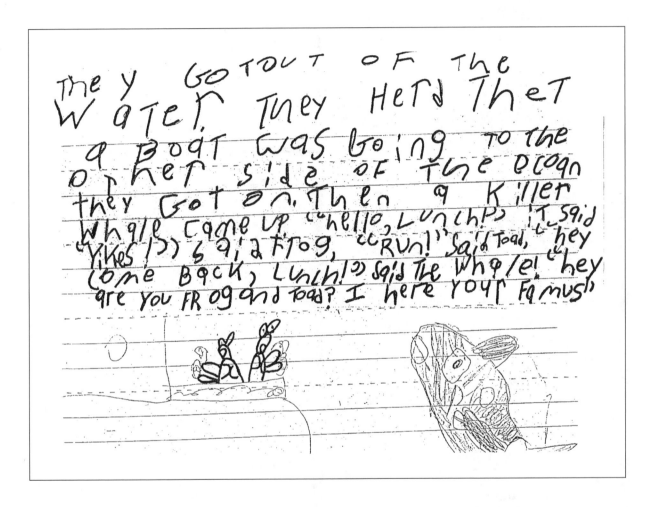

They got out of the water. They heard that a boat was going to the other side of the ocean. They got on. Then a killer whale came up.

"Hello, lunch!" it said.

"Yikes," said Frog.

"Run!" said Toad.

"Hey, come back, lunch!" said the whale. "Hey, are you Frog and Toad? I hear you're famous."

Rhyming Words

→ **EMERGENT**
DEVELOPING
INDEPENDENT

Little Miss Muffet
Mother Goose
Nursery Rhyme

Little Miss Muffet
Sat on a tuffet
Eating her curds and whey
Along came a spider
And sat down beside her
And frightened Miss Muffet away

Activities

Write the nursery rhyme on chart paper, leaving off the last word in each sentence. Make a small slit on the chart where the missing word should be. Put in a paper clip and tape the back of it to the chart. Put the last words on cards. As you are reading the chart, have students come up and put in the last word.

Little Miss ⬚ Muffet

Sat on a ⬚ tuffet

Eating her curds and ⬚ whey

Along came a ⬚

And sat down beside ⬚

And frightened Miss Muffet ⬚

Literature Extensions

Make a class big book changing a line of the nursery rhyme.

> Little Miss Muffet
> Sat on a tuffet
> Eating her curds and whey
> Along came a _____

Students can make pictures of what came along. But whatever comes along has to have words that rhyme with it:
    Along came a(n)

> dark lark
> boy with toy
> king with a ring

The last page will say:

> And frightened Miss Muffet away.

CAT
Who was wearing a hat,

Rhyming Words

EMERGENT
→ **DEVELOPING**
INDEPENDENT

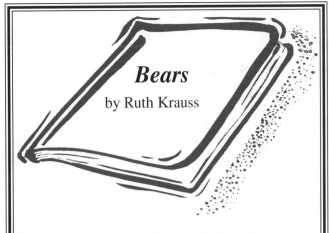

Bears
by Ruth Krauss

Bears is a short, rhyming book about bears. Each page tells what bears do, such as: washing hairs, giving stares, collecting fares

Activities

Find all of the words that rhyme with bears:

stairs	millionaires	chairs
fares	hairs	squares
stares		

Brainstorm other words that rhyme.

Literature Extensions

Create a new big book about another animal and follow the same repetitive, rhyming pattern:

Sharks, sharks, sharks, sharks, sharks
  Walking in parks
  As happy as larks
  Correcting tests and giving marks
    or
Raccoons, raccoons, raccoons, raccoons,
  Eating with spoons
  Looking at moons
  Sailing in balloons

 Other suggested resources:

Jesse Bear, What Will You Wear? by Nancy
  White Carlstrom
Who's Sick Today? by Lynne Cherry
All Nursery Rhymes
See You Later Alligator . . .
  by Barbara Strauss and Helen Friedland
Squeeze a Sneeze by Bill Morrison
The Missing Tarts by B.G. Hennessy

Rhyming Words

EMERGENT

DEVELOPING

➜ **INDEPENDENT**

One Sun, a Book of Terse Verse has two rhyming words with illustrations on each page.

Activities

We look at rhyming words every week. As a class, we brainstorm all of the words we can think of that contain our spelling pattern for the week.

For example, if our spelling pattern is **ai**, then students will brainstorm all of the words that have that pattern. We usually get words that rhyme but are spelled differently. This becomes a mini-lesson.

In *One Sun*, all of the words rhyme, but many are spelled differently. As you read each page, have students generate a list of rhyming words. Write them down as students are brainstorming, and have students categorize them into spelling patterns.

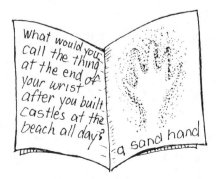

What would you call the thing at the end of your wrist after you built castles at the beach all day? a sand hand

Literature Extensions

Students can make their own book of "terse verse" by following the same pattern as in *One Sun*.

Create some Hink Pinks. Use *One Sun* as the basis to practice making the rhymes:

What would you call a rock that is all by itself?
a lone stone

What would you call a tiny, round object?
a small ball

What would you call your dog after it fell into the water?
a wet pet

I found it easier for students to think of a pair of rhyming words first and then the question.

Sequencing

→ **EMERGENT**
DEVELOPING
INDEPENDENT

Sight Vocabulary

Charlie   he

Charlie Needs a Cloak is a story about a shepherd who needs a new cloak for the winter. The book describes how he went about making the cloak.

Activities

Make the following cards for students to put in order. Copy some pictures to glue onto the cards.

Charlie sheared his sheep.	He washed the wool.
He carded the wool to straighten it.	He spun the wool into yarn
He picked pokeweed berries and boiled them.	He dyed the yarn red.
He wove the yarn into cloth.	He cut the cloth into pieces.
He pinned and then sewed the pieces.	Charlie had a new cloak.

Literature Extensions

Students can make how-to books. Give students a sheep shape to trace and cut out as a cover for their book. Students can draw pictures to retell the sequence of events that happened in the story. Depending on your students' abilities, they can write, or you can do the writing for them.

Make other how-to books. Brainstorm with students all of the things they know how to do: make a sandwich, ride a bike, play ball, etc.

Have them make books. Some might do all illustrations, some might add text, or the teacher can add the text.

This sample was done by a special needs child who is at the beginning developing reading stage:

How to Play Baseball

You Shud hold The Bat rit in Basbal. You haf to be god
1. Pick up the bat
2. StupTo The bos
3. Swin The Bat

Sequencing

EMERGENT
➡ **DEVELOPING**
INDEPENDENT

Sight Vocabulary

farmer	hat	brown	said
the	saw		

Who Took the Farmer's Hat?

by Joan Nodset

This story is about a farmer's hat that gets blown off his head by the wind and ends up in many funny places.

Activities

Bring in an old brown hat and act out the story.

Talk about the wind. Discuss what things, other than the farmer's hat, that the wind can blow away or move.

For example:
    trees
    plants
    flowers
    clothes on a clothesline
    clothes on people
    hair

Using the interactive chart, students put the sentence strips in order.

The wind blew off the farmer's hat.

The squirrel saw a fat, round bird in the sky.

Mouse saw a big, round mousehole.

Literature Extensions

Students can write or illustrate the following:

What else could have happened to the hat? Where could it have gone? What other animals could have seen it, and what did they mistake it for?

Sequencing

EMERGENT

DEVELOPING

➜ **INDEPENDENT**

Hot-Air Henry

by Mary Calhoun

Hot-Air Henry is about a cat who takes off in a hot-air balloon.

Activities

Take a piece of chart or mural paper and fold it into eighths. Have students write or illustrate the story in sequence using the eight boxes.

The woman and instructor are getting the balloon ready.	Henry races to stow away and the balloon takes off.	He sails toward the mountains.	The basket comes down and bounces up again.
Henry encounters some blackbirds.	He meets an eagle.	He meets some geese.	The basket lands.

After completing this activity, cut the paper apart into the eight boxes. Students can put the pictures and/or text back in the correct order.

Lay the boxes out on the floor in a different sequence than the story. Does the story still make sense? What events could have happened in a different sequence while still keeping the story line?

Add some boxes with new adventures for Henry.

Literature Extensions

Students can do a lot of different writing activities:

What other adventures could Henry have had while up in the hot-air balloon?

If you could go anywhere in a hot-air balloon, where would you go and why?

Create a story about your adventures in a hot-air balloon.

Other books written about Henry include: *Cross Country Cat, High-Wire Henry,* and *Henry the Sailor Cat.*

What other adventures besides ballooning, sailing, and skiing could Henry have? Write about one.

Similes

EMERGENT
DEVELOPING
→ **INDEPENDENT**

Quick as
a Cricket

by Audrey Wood

Quick as a Cricket is a beautiful picture book that has similes on every page.

Activities

Talk about similes. What are they? How and why are they used?

Rewrite the text to *Quick as a Cricket* using other comparison words. For example, instead of saying:

I'm as small as an ant, brainstorm with students all of the other words they could use instead of ant: crumb, gnat, mosquito, seed, baby's fingernail, etc. Do this for each page of the book.

Have your students visit a younger class and teach them what similes are. My class taught their kindergarten pen pals. The younger students then made a class book. The kindergartners drew the pictures and told the older students what to write.

Literature Extensions

Students can create their own books that describe themselves through the use of similes, as in the book *Quick as a Cricket*. Students can refer to the brainstormed lists of comparisons to help them.

Some examples my students came up with are:

> as warm as my blanket
> as loud as a police siren
> as hot as a fire

Have student pick an object or animal and describe it using similes.

Story Elements

➔ **EMERGENT**
DEVELOPING
INDEPENDENT

Three Billy Goats Gruff

This story is about three goats that need to cross a bridge in order to eat some grass on the other side. The bridge is being guarded by a troll who will not let them pass.

Activities

Talk about the story elements. As students come up with ideas, write them on chart paper.

Characters: three goats, troll

Setting: outside, near a meadow and a bridge

Problem: The goats want to cross the bridge, but the troll won't let them.

Plot: As each goat gets to the bridge, it tells the troll to wait for the next goat because it is bigger and fatter.

Resolution: The goats all get to the other side and get rid of the troll.

Literature Extensions

Students can make storyboards. (See pages 9-13 for examples of different kinds of storyboards.)

Story Elements

EMERGENT
➡ **DEVELOPING**
INDEPENDENT

Why Can't I Fly?
by
Rita Golden Gelman

This story is about a monkey named Minnie who wants to fly. She seeks the advice of her animal friends who can fly. Her friends tell her that in order to fly she must have a certain attribute that they have.

Sight Vocabulary

goodbye	can	can't
climbed	fly	

Activities

Make a transparency of Story Elements (page 104) and/or Event Map (page 103).

Put the transparencies on the overhead and fill them out with students. Talk about the different story elements. Have students try to define each element.

My students love these activities because they like writing on the board. The transparencies make the format appear very large on the board.

 Other suggested resources:

Strega Nona by Tomie dePaola
The Ugly Duckling by Hans Christian Anderson

Literature Extensions

Students can choose another book they are reading or have read and complete their own story element sheet and/or event map.

After students have completed either the story elements sheet or event map, have them change one of the elements.

How will the story change?
What could remain the same?
What would have to be different?

Sample:

Story Elements

Name: _____

Title: _____Why Can't I Fly?_____

Author: _____Rita Golden Gelman_____

Setting: ___in the woods, near a tree, and near water_____

_____

Characters: ___Minnie, bluebird, yellow bird, ladybug, duck, butterfly___

_____

Plot: ___Minnie talks to her friends who can fly and they give her advice. All__
___of the advice has to do with each animal's attribute. For example,___
___the duck says she has to have feathers.___

Conflict/Problem: ___Minnie is a monkey who wants to fly, but she is___
___having difficulty learning.___

Resolution/Solution: ___Minnie's friends catch her in a sheet and fly her___
___through the air.___

Event Map

Name: _____

Title: Why Can't I Fly?

Author: Rita Golden Gelman

Setting/Characters:

Setting: Outside in the woods, near a tree and near water
Characters: Minnie, bluebird, yellow bird, ladybug, duck, butterfly

Problem:

Minnie is a monkey and she wants to fly, but she is not being successful.

Event 1

Minnie meets two birds and they try to help her fly. They tell her she needs to get rid of her boots and sing a song.

Event 2

Minnie meets a ladybug who tells Minnie she needs spots in order to fly.

Event 3

Minnie meets a duck. The duck tells Minnie that she needs feathers in order to fly.

Event 4

Minnie meets a butterfly that tells Minnie she needs wings in order to fly.

Solution/Resolution:

Her friends put her on a sheet and fly her across the sky.

Event Map

Name: _____

Title: _____

Author: _____

Setting/Characters:

Problem:

Event 1

Event 2

Event 3

Event 4

Solution/Resolution:

Story Elements

Name: _____

Title: _____

Author: _____

Setting: _____

_____

_____

Characters: _____

_____

_____

Plot: _____

_____

_____

Conflict/Problem: _____

_____

_____

Resolution/Solution: _____

_____

_____

Story Elements

EMERGENT

DEVELOPING

➡ **INDEPENDENT**

Zella, Zack and Zodiac

by Bill Peet

This story is about a zebra named Zella who takes in Zack, an orphaned ostrich, who eventually becomes indispensable to Zella.

Activities

Discuss the story elements in this book. Record students' responses using a large piece of mural paper cut out in the shape of a zebra.

Setting: the African plains
Students need to think about where zebras, lions, leopards, and acacia trees are found.

Characters: Zella, Zack, and Zodiac

Plot: A zebra named Zella takes in an orphaned ostrich named Zack, who grows up and lives with the zebra herd. Zella has a baby named Zodiac, who is always finding himself in trouble. Zack repays Zella by being there to take care of Zodiac, her clumsy baby.

Students can think of the plot as being a kind of summary.

Conflict/Problem: 1. A baby ostrich is abandoned by his mother and needs a home. 2. Zodiac has gigantic hoofs and is always finding himself in precarious situations.

Resolution/Solution: 1. Zella and the zebra herd adopt Zack. 2. Zack watches over Zodiac until he grows up to fit his feet.

Literature Extensions

How would the story change if the story elements were different? Have students think about this question and write about the changes. For example, what if . . . .

Zella never took the ostrich in?
Zella took the ostrich in but the
     other zebras did not accept it?
Zack had a different personality?

There are many other great books by Bill Peet. Students can read another book and then write about the story elements on a piece of mural paper cut out in the shape of something that is important to the story.

Books written by Bill Peet include:

The Caboose That Got Loose
Cowardly Clyde
Chester the Worldly Pig
The Whingdingdilly
How Droofus the Dragon Lost His Head

Verb Ending: ed

EMERGENT
➡ **DEVELOPING**
INDEPENDENT

The Big Sneeze
by Ruth Brown

One hot afternoon a farmer and his animals decide to take a nap. A fly lands on the farmer's nose, making him sneeze. A comical series of events follows.

Activities

Students brainstorm all of the verbs with the **ed** ending:

stopped	landed	sneezed
disturbed	captured	alerted
chased	wakened	replied
shrieked	scattered	startled
panicked	frightened	

Make an "Ending Rule" chart (see next page).

Put all of the words into a hat. Have students come up one at a time and act out each verb.

Have students brainstorm synonyms for the verbs:

panicked — terrified, scared, frightened

shrieked — screamed, yelled, stammered, cried

captured — caught, seized, grasped

Talk about how the endings of these new verbs were formed. Add them to the chart.

Literature Extensions

Students can make their own versions of *The Big Sneeze*. What other chain of events might have happened when the farmer sneezed?

What might have happened if a giant sneezed?

Have students think about a chain of events that has happened to them and write about it. For example:

> dinner was cooking . . . .
> the phone rang . . . .
> talked too long . . . .
> dinner burned . . . .
> raced to oven . . . .
> tripped over cat . . . .
> cat screamed . . . .
> dog barked . . . . , etc.

 Other suggested resource:

Which Witch Is Which? by Pat Hutchins

Verb Ending: ed

EMERGENT

DEVELOPING

➜ **INDEPENDENT**

The House That Jack Built
illustrated by
Jenny Stow

This is a cumulative tale. Each page repeats the episode and adds another. The illustrations put this Mother Goose rhyme in the Caribbean.

Activities

Find all of the words with an **ed** ending and write them on the board or on chart paper. Have students look at the words and generate some rules about what happens to words when an ending is added. Categorize the words from the book and add more.

Final E	Consonant Y	No changes
waked hoped	worried married carried	killed tossed milked kissed crowed

I find if I leave charts like this up, students often use them to help with spelling patterns. Also, when new rules come up, students immediately go to the charts where a new category should be added — for example, doubling the final consonant before adding **ed**.

Literature Extensions

Students can make their own versions, *The House That* (student's name) *Built*.

Students should use at least two verbs from each of the different categories (the spelling patterns, not necessarily the verbs themselves).

Have students look through another book they are reading and list some verbs. Then have them make a chart and categorize the verbs according to rules for adding **ed**.

Verb Ending: ing

EMERGENT
→ **DEVELOPING**
INDEPENDENT

Polar Bear, Polar Bear, What Do You Hear?
by Bill Martin Jr.

This is a predictable, repetitive book. Animals are asked what they hear and each responds with another animal's name and the sound it makes.

Sight Vocabulary

what	do	you	hear
in	my	ear	

Activities

Point out words with the **ing** ending on each page in the book. Mask the **ing** ending and read the book again.

List other verbs that also have an **ing** ending — jump-jumping, climb-climbing, read-reading, etc.

Make signs for students to wear. Write the verbs that were used in the story without the **ing** ending: roar, snort, flute, bray, hiss, etc. Make signs that have words plus the **ing** endings. Students can pair up to make hiss-hissing and bray-braying, etc.

Point out to students the two words that have a different pattern (whistle-whistling and flute-fluting).

Discuss the sounds other animals make. Chart students' ideas:
    horse — neighing
    dog — barking
    monkey — chattering
    duck — quacking, etc.

Literature Extensions

Make a new class big book and use the new animals and their sounds that students brainstormed during the activity.

Make a class big book about sounds you would hear in the classroom:

> Teacher, teacher, what do you hear?
> I hear Jim's watch ticking in my ear.
>
> Jim, Jim, what do you hear?
> I hear water dripping in my ear.
>
> Sally, Sally, what do you hear?
> I hear a fire drill screeching in my ear.

Verb Ending: ing

EMERGENT
➡ **DEVELOPING**
INDEPENDENT

Sight Vocabulary

caught	it	picked	up
put	in	cage	then
little	was	saw	

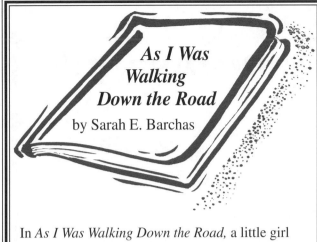

As I Was Walking Down the Road by Sarah E. Barchas

In *As I Was Walking Down the Road*, a little girl finds different animals and puts each one into a cage. At the end of the story, she sets them free.

Activities

Find all the words that have an **ing** ending: walking, looking, working, jumping, cleaning, waiting, sweeping, eating, reading, pushing.

Put all these words on index cards. Have students take turns picking a card and acting out what it says.

Have students brainstorm things they like to do. Write down their responses. Have students come up and underline or circle the **ing** endings.

Other suggested resources:

Brown Bear Brown Bear, What Do You See? by Bill Martin Jr.
Things I Like by Anthony Browne
Possum Come a-Knockin' by Nancy Van Laan

Literature Extensions

Make a class book. Using the same repetitive story line, students can be doing different things and finding different animals.

Students can refer to the list of verbs they brainstormed during the activity time to get them started.

Verb Ending: ing

EMERGENT

DEVELOPING

➔ **INDEPENDENT**

Have You Seen Birds?
by
Joanne Oppenheim
and Barbara Reed

This book is written in prose. It describes many different kinds of birds and what they can do.

Activities

This book has a wealth of verbs. Have students find all of the words with the **ing** ending and write them on the board. Have them find the root words and make generalizations about rules for adding the **ing** ending.

Make a rule chart.

No Changes	Double Final Consonant	Drop Final E
cheeping	snapping	leaving
sleeping	tapping	coming
peeping	rapping	freezing
eating	strutting	piping
pulling	skimming	scaring
drinking	chatting	whistling
singing	dipping	paddling
splashing		wading
visiting		diving
following		gliding
searching		racing
quarreling		

These are only some of the verbs found in this book!

Literature Extensions

Have students choose an animal and brainstorm with them all of the things it can do. For example:

> Cats:
> purring, eating, meowing, crying, rubbing, cleaning, stalking, hunting, etc.

> Dogs
> barking, protecting, jumping, fetching, swimming, paddling, etc.

Students can make their own books about the animal they picked.

Vowel Pattern: Long A Sound

EMERGENT
➡ **DEVELOPING**
INDEPENDENT

Is Your Mama a Llama?
by Deborah Guarino

This is a predictable, repetitive story about a baby llama who visits his friends and asks them about their mama.

Activities

Students brainstorm all of the words from the book with the long **a** sound: Dave, gave, cave, behave, explained, say, grazes, day, way. Make a chart of the three ways to spell long **a**. Students try to add as many words as they can under each category.

a_e	ai	ay
Dave	explained	day
gave		way
cave	paint	
behave	rain	play
grazes	maid	tray
	grain	Monday
save		Tuesday
bake		clay
came		

Literature Extensions

What other friends could the baby llama meet?

Have students work individually or in pairs and write another verse to *Is Your Mama a Llama?* Students could choose animals that have something in common. For example:

circus animals
sea animals
animals becoming extinct
warm blooded/cold blooded
farm animals

Vowel Pattern: Long E Sound

EMERGENT
➜ **DEVELOPING**
INDEPENDENT

Polar Bear, Polar Bear, What Do You Hear?
by Bill Martin Jr.

Polar Bear, Polar Bear, What Do You Hear?
is a predictable, repetitive book. Animals are
asked what they hear; each responds with
another animal's name and the sound it makes.

Sight Vocabulary

hear	ear	in	my
what	do	you	

Activities

Students brainstorm all of the words from
the book with the long **e** sound: me, see,
green, sheep, ear, hear. Make a chart of
the three ways to spell long **e**. Students try
to add as many words as they can under
each category.

e	ee	ea
be	sheep	hear
	green	fear
	tree	near
	feet	bean
	meet	beak
	jeep	seal

Literature Extensions

Students can make
I See _____ books.

They can fill in the blank with one, two, or
more words. At least one of the words has to
have a long **e** sound. Students can make up
nonsense sentences.

I see three green fleas on my feet!

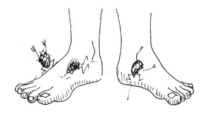

Students can make their own books using the
same repetitive pattern but incorporating a
science or social studies theme.

Ocean, Ocean, what do you hear?
I hear a wave splashing in my ear.
Wave, Wave, what do you hear?
I hear a dolphin whistling in my ear.

Vowel Pattern: Long E Sound

EMERGENT
→ **DEVELOPING**
INDEPENDENT

Sight Vocabulary

I   the   we   all

*Peep's
Diary*

by John Astrop

Peep's Diary is about a chick who keeps a diary about what he did last week. He writes down one thing he did each day.

Activities

Students brainstorm all the words from the book that have a long **e** sound:

Peep, week, Beesley, we, beach

Add these words to a chart of long **e** words (see page 112).

Literature Extensions

Make a list of all the things Peep could have done during the week that have a long **e** sound.

> play in his tree house
> sleep until noon
> play hide and go seek
> drink some tea

Students can illustrate their favorite one and display on a bulletin board, or they can be put together in a class book.

Look at the chart of long **e** words on page 112. Students can make a new diary for Peep using words on the chart. What new adventures will he have this week?

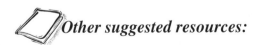 *Other suggested resources:*

Hailstones and Halibut Bones by Mary O'Neill ("What Is Green?")
Crackers and Crumbs by Sonja Dunn ("Different Days," page 48, poem with long e spelled y at end of words)
Where the Sidewalk Ends by Shel Silverstein ("Treehouse," page 79)

Vowel Pattern: Long I Sound

EMERGENT
➡️ **DEVELOPING**
INDEPENDENT

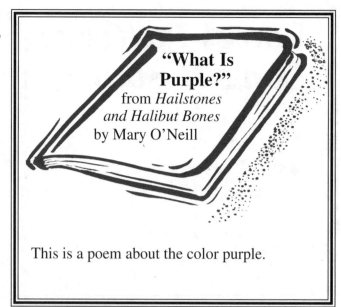

"What Is Purple?"
from *Hailstones and Halibut Bones*
by Mary O'Neill

This is a poem about the color purple.

Sight Vocabulary

purple

Activities

Students brainstorm all the words from the book that have a long **i** sound in the poem. Then they brainstorm any other words they can think of. Write down the words as students say them. Have students categorize the spelling patterns.

ight	i_e	_y
night	time	fly
bright	fire	my
light	hire	cry
sight		

Literature Extensions

Have students think about all the things that are purple. What does purple make them think of? How does purple make them feel? Make up a master sheet like the following for students to organize their ideas:

Purple	
smells like...	looks like...
feels like...	makes me think of...

Have students write their own purple poems and illustrate using purple finger paint or different crayon shades of purple.

 Other suggested resources:

Alligator Pie by Dennis Lee,
("Alligator Pie," page 8, first verse)
Star Light Star Bright (poem)
The New Kid on the Block by Jack
Prelutsky, ("Nine Mice," page 9)

Vowel Pattern: Long O Sound

EMERGENT

➔ **DEVELOPING**

INDEPENDENT

"Joey"
from *Where the Sidewalk Ends*
by Shel Silverstein

This is a silly poem about a boy named Joey who threw a stone at the sun and knocked it down.

Sight Vocabulary

wouldn't   night
down

Activities

Students brainstorm all of the words from the book with the long **o** sound: stone, toe, grow, blow, crow, Joe. Make a chart of three ways to spell long **o**. Students try to add as many words as they can under each category.

You can add the spelling pattern **oa** and have students brainstorm words with that pattern.

Literature Extensions

Using the words on the chart for some ideas, students can think about other silly things that could never happen. They can make up their own silly poems and then illustrate them. Put all of the poems together in a class book of nonsense poems.

o_e	ow	oe	oa
stone	**blow** **grow** **crow**	**Joe** **toe**	
note	tow		goat
quote	snow		foam
stove	glow		boat
close			coach
vote			toad
nose			coal

Vowel Pattern: OO Sound

(as in raccoon)

EMERGENT
➡ **DEVELOPING**
INDEPENDENT

Sight Vocabulary

the   and

Hey Diddle Diddle
Mother Goose
Nursery Rhyme

Hey diddle diddle
The cat and the fiddle
The cow jumped over the moon
The little dog laughed
To see such sport
And the dish ran away
With the spoon

Activities

Find the words with the **oo** pattern in the nursery rhyme. Then have students brainstorm as many other words as they can that have the **oo** sound.

balloon	moon
soon	raccoon
noon	spoon
food	fool
moose	pool
tool	tooth
zoo	goose

Make some 3-D cards of the **oo** pattern (see next page).

Literature Extensions

Make a class big book changing a line of the nursery rhyme. The first page will say:

Hey diddle diddle
The cat and the fiddle

Students can create their own pages of what went over the moon.

The last page will read:

The little dog laughed
To see such sport
And the dish ran away with the spoon.

Vowel Pattern: OR Sound

EMERGENT
➔ **DEVELOPING**
INDEPENDENT

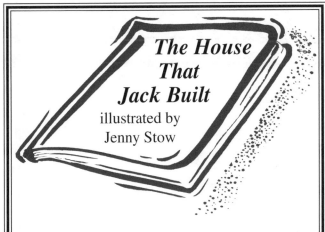

The House That Jack Built
illustrated by Jenny Stow

This is a cumulative tale. Each page repeats the episode and adds another. The illustrations puts this Mother Goose rhyme in the Caribbean.

Activities

Find words with the **or** pattern.

horn, forlorn, torn, shorn, morn, corn

Have students brainstorm other words with the **or** sound.

Make some 3" x 5" oaktag strips or use unlined index cards. Write **or** on the cards with colored glue. When it dries, you will have a raised 3-D effect of the **or** pattern. Have students make rubbings of the pattern and then add letters with a pencil or crayon to make words.

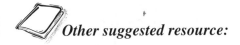

Other suggested resource:

Little Boy Blue Mother Goose Nursery Rhyme

Literature Extensions

Students can create their own books titled:

The House That (student's name) *Built.*

As students are writing, they need to include words with the **or** pattern on each page. They can refer to the list they brainstormed during activity time to help them.

Vowel Pattern: OW Sound

(as in down)

EMERGENT
➡ **DEVELOPING**
INDEPENDENT

"Turkey Time" from *Crackers and Crumbs* by Sonja Dunn

Sight Vocabulary

the   and

Activities

Put this poem on a chart and laminate it so students can write on it and wipe it off. If you don't have access to a laminating machine, take two pieces of clear contact paper, large enough to lay over the chart. Stick them together. Now you have a sheet of plastic to lay over any chart or poster you have!

Students can circle all of the **ow** words.

down, town, frown, brown

Have students generate a list of other words with the same sound. Students may think of words that have the **ou** pattern like the word couch. Write all of the suggestions down and then categorize them by pattern.

 Other suggested resource:

Butterscotch Dreams by Sonja Dunn
    ("All the Crowds," page 21)

Literature Extensions

Using the words generated in the activity, have students make up their own poems or nonsense sentences.

The brown owl howled and growled.

The king wore his brown crown to owl's birthday party.

Bibliography

Children's Bibliography

As you look through the lists of books I've suggested for emergent, developing, and independent readers, you'll notice that some books appear on more than one list. Some of these books may be beyond students' ability to read independently but are great read-alouds. On the other hand, some may appear easy for students. As I've mentioned earlier, I use books students can read comfortably to teach skills because I want them to focus on learning the skill without getting bogged down in reading the text.

Books Especially Good for Emergent Readers

Ahlberg, Janet and Allan. *Each Peach Pear Plum*. New York: Viking, 1979.

Allen, Pamela. *Who Sank the Boat?* New York: Coward-McCann, 1983.

Astrop, John. *Peep's Diary*. New York: Gallery Books, 1986.

Browne, Anthony. *Things I Like*. New York: Knopf, 1989.

Burningham, John. *Mr. Gumpy's Outing*. Weston, CT: Weston Woods, 1973.

Carle, Eric. *The Mixed-up Chameleon*. New York: Scholastic, 1975.

———. *The Very Busy Spider*. New York: Philomel, 1984.

Carter, David. *How Many Bugs in a Box?* New York: Simon & Schuster, 1988.

Cherry, Lynne. *Who's Sick Today?* New York: Dutton, 1988.

Christelow, Eileen. *Five Little Monkeys Jumping on the Bed*. New York: Clarion Books, 1988.

Cole, Joanna. *Animal Sleepyheads 1 to 10*. New York: Scholastic, 1988.

Crews, Donald. *Freight Train*. New York: Scholastic, 1989.

dePaola, Tomie. *Charlie Needs a Cloak*. New York: Simon and Schuster, 1973.

Dodds, Dayle Ann. *Wheel Away!* New York: Scholastic, 1989.

Ehlert, Lois. *Planting a Rainbow*. New York: Harcourt Brace & Company, 1988.

Freeman, Don. *Corduroy*. New York: Scholastic, 1968.

Galdone, Paul. *The Gingerbread Boy*. New York: Clarion, 1975.

Gelman, Rita Golden. *More Spaghetti I Say*. New York: Scholastic, 1984.

———. *Why Can't I Fly?* New York: Scholastic, 1976.

Handy, Libby. *Boss for a Week*. New York: Scholastic.

Henkes, Kevin. *Chrysanthemum*. New York: Greenwillow, 1991.

Hennessy, B.G. *The Missing Tarts*. New York: Scholastic, 1989.

Hoban, Tana. *Of Colors and Things*. New York: Scholastic, 1989.

Hooper, Meredith. *Seven Eggs*. London: Patrick Hardy Books, 1985.

Hutchins, Pat. *Rosie's Walk*. New York: Scholastic, 1987.

————. *The Doorbell Rang*. New York: Scholastic, 1986.

Kalan, Robert. *Jump, Frog, Jump!* New York: Greenwillow, 1981.

————. *Rain*. New York: Macmillan/McGraw-Hill, 1978.

Krauss, Ruth. *Bears*. New York: Scholastic, 1948.

Martin, Bill Jr. *Brown Bear, Brown Bear, What Do You See?* New York: Holt, 1983.

————. *Polar Bear, Polar Bear, What Do You Hear?* New York: Holt, 1991.

Morrison, Bill. *Squeeze a Sneeze*. New York: Houghton Mifflin, 1977.

Noble, Trinka Hakes. *Jimmy's Boa and the Big Splash Birthday Bash*. New York: Penguin Books, 1989.

————. *The Day Jimmy's Boa Ate the Wash*. New York: Dial Books, 1980.

Nodset, Joan L. *Who Took the Farmer's Hat?* New York: Scholastic, 1963.

Numeroff, Laura Joffe. *If You Give a Moose a Muffin*. New York: HarperCollins, 1991.

————. *If You Give a Mouse a Cookie*. New York: Harper & Row, 1985.

Peek, Merle. *Mary Wore Her Red Dress and Henry Wore His Green Sneakers*. New York: Clarion, 1985.

————. *The Balancing Act: A Counting Book*. New York: Clarion, 1987.

Samton, Sheila White. *Beside the Bay*. New York: Philomel, 1987.

Shaw, Charles G. *It Looked Like Spilt Milk*. New York: Harper & Row, 1947.

Steig, William. *Sylvester and the Magic Pebble*. New York: Simon & Schuster, 1969.

Strauss, Barbara, and Friedland, Helen. *See You Later Alligator*. Los Angeles: Price Stern Sloan, 1986.

Turkle, Brinton. *Deep in the Forest*. New York: Dutton, 1976.

Ward, Cindy. *Cookie's Week*. New York: Putnam, 1988.

Wells, Rosemary. *Noisy Nora*. New York: Dial, 1973.

Wood, Audrey. *The Napping House*. San Diego: Harcourt Brace Jovanovich, 1984.

Plus these traditional stories:

Goldilocks and the Three Bears
Little Red Hen, The
Three Billy Goats Gruff

Books Especially Good for Developing Readers

Ahlberg, Janet and Allan. *Each Peach Pear Plum*. New York: Viking, 1979.

Allard, Harry. *It's So Nice to Have a Wolf Around the House*. New York: Doubleday, 1977.

Allen, Pamela. *Mr. Archimedes' Bath*. New York: Angus & Robertson, 1980.

Anderson, Hans Christian. *The Ugly Duckling*. New York: Scholastic, 1987.

Astrop, John. *Peep's Diary*. New York: Gallery Books, 1986.

Barchas, Sarah E. *I Was Walking Down the Road*. New York: Scholastic, 1975.

Bouchard, David. *My Little Pigs*. Winnipeg, Manitoba: Whole Language Consultants, 1991.

Brett, Jan. *The Mitten*. New York: Putnam, 1989.

Brown, Ruth. *The Big Sneeze*. New York: Shepard Books, 1985.

Browne, Anthony. *Things I Like*. New York: Knopf, 1989.

Cameron, Polly. *I Can't Said the Ant*. New York: Scholastic, 1989.

Carle, Eric. *The Mixed-up Chameleon*. New York: Scholastic, 1975.

———. *Today Is Monday*. New York: Philomel, 1993.

———. *The Very Hungry Caterpillar*. New York: Philomel, 1969.

Carlstrom, Nancy White. *Jesse Bear, What Will You Wear?* New York: Macmillan, 1986.

Celsi, Teresa. *The Fourth Little Pig*. Austin, TX: Steck-Vaughn, 1992.

Cherry, Lynne. *Who's Sick Today?* New York: Dutton, 1988.

Climo, Shirley. *The Egyptian Cinderella*. New York: Crowell, 1989.

Crews, Donald. *Freight Train*. New York: Scholastic, 1989.

dePaola, Tomie. *Strega Nona*. Englewood Cliffs, NJ: Prentice-Hall, 1975.

Dodds, Dayle Ann. *Wheel Away!* New York: Scholastic, 1989.

Duke, Kate. *Guinea Pigs Far and Near*. New York: Dutton, 1984.

Freeman, Don. *Corduroy*. New York: Scholastic, 1968.

Galdone, Paul. *The Gingerbread Boy*. New York: Clarion, 1975.

Gelman, Rita Golden. *More Spaghetti I Say*. New York: Scholastic, 1984.

———. *Why Can't I Fly?* New York: Scholastic, 1976.

Guarino, Deborah. *Is Your Mama a Llama?* New York: Scholastic, 1989.

Handy, Libby. *Boss for a Week*. New York: Scholastic.

Henkes, Kevin. *Chrysanthemum*. New York: Greenwillow, 1991.

Hennessy, B.G. *The Missing Tarts*. New York: Scholastic, 1989.

Hoban, Tana. *Over, Under and Through*. New York: Aladdin Books, 1987.

Hooper, Meredith. *Seven Eggs*. London: Patrick Hardy Books, 1985.

Huck, Charlotte, and Lobel, Anita. *Princess Furball*. New York: Scholastic, 1989.

Hutchins, Pat. *Rosie's Walk*. New York: Scholastic, 1987.

———. *The Doorbell Rang*. New York: Scholastic, 1986.

———. *Which Witch Is Which?* New York: Greenwillow, 1989.

Kalan, Robert. *Rain*. New York: Macmillan/McGraw-Hill, 1978.

Krauss, Ruth. *Bears*. New York: Scholastic, 1948.

Lester, Helen. *Tacky the Penguin*. Boston: Houghton Mifflin, 1988.

Lionni, Leo. *It's Mine*. New York: Knopf, 1986.

Louie, Ai-Ling. *Yeh-Shen*. New York: Philomel, 1986.

Lowell, Susan. *The Three Little Javelinas*. Flagstaff, AZ: Northland Publishing, 1992.

Lyon, George Ella. *Together*. New York: Orchard Books, 1989.

Martin, Bill Jr. *Brown Bear, Brown Bear, What Do You See?* New York: Holt, 1983.

———. *Polar Bear, Polar Bear, What Do You Hear?* New York: Holt, 1991.

Martin, Rafe, and Shannon, David. *The Rough-Face Girl*. New York: Putnam, 1992.

Mathews, Louise. *Cluck One*. Northbrook, IL: Dodd Mead, 1982.

McMillan, Bruce. *One Sun*. New York: Scholastic, 1990.

Morrison, Bill. *Squeeze a Sneeze*. New York: Houghton Mifflin, 1977.

Noble, Trinka Hakes. *The Day Jimmy's Boa Ate the Wash*. New York: Dial Books, 1980.

———. *Jimmy's Boa and the Big Splash Birthday Bash*. New York: Penguin Books, 1989.

Nodset, Joan L. *Who Took the Farmer's Hat?* New York: Scholastic, 1963.

Numeroff, Laura Joffe. *If You Give a Moose a Muffin*. New York: HarperCollins, 1991.

———. *If You Give a Mouse a Cookie*. New York: Harper & Row, 1985.

Oppenheim, Joanne, and Reid, Barbara. *Have You Seen Birds?* New York: Scholastic, 1986.

Peek, Merle. *Mary Wore Her Red Dress and Henry Wore His Green Sneakers*. New York: Clarion, 1985.

Perrault, Charles. *Cinderella*. New York: Dial Books, 1985.

Raschka, Chris. *Yo! Yes?* New York: Orchard Books, 1993.

Samton, Sheila White. *Beside the Bay*. New York: Philomel, 1987.

Scieszka, Jon. *The True Story of the Three Pigs* (as told by A. Wolf). New York: Viking, 1989.

Serfozo, Mary. *Who Said Red?* New York: McElderry Books, 1987.

Slobodkina, Esphyr. *Caps for Sale*. New York: Harper & Row, 1968.

Steig, William. *Sylvester and the Magic Pebble*. New York: Simon & Schuster, 1969.

Steptoe, John. *Mufaro's Beautiful Daughters*. New York: Lothrop, Lee, & Shepard, 1987.

Stow, Jenny (illustrator). *The House That Jack Built*. New York: Dial Books, 1992.

Strauss, Barbara, and Friedland, Helen. *See You Later Alligator.* Los Angeles: Price Stern Sloan, 1986.

Turkle, Brinton. *Deep in the Forest*. New York: Dutton, 1976.

Van Laan, Nancy. *Possum Come a-Knockin'*. New York: Dragonfly Books, 1990.

Ward, Cindy. *Cookie's Week*. New York: Putnam, 1988.

Wood, Audrey. *Quick as a Cricket*. Clarkston, MI: Child's Play, 1982.

———. *The Napping House*. San Diego: Harcourt Brace Jovanovich, 1984.

Young, Ed. *Lon Po Po*. New York: Philomel, 1989.

Plus these traditional stories:

Goldilocks and the Three Bears
Little Red Hen, The
Little Red Riding Hood
Three Billy Goats Gruff
Three Little Pigs, The

Books Especially Good for Independent Readers

Adler, David. *Cam Jansen and the Mystery of the Dinosaur Bones*. New York: Scholastic, 1980.

Ahlberg, Janet and Allan. *Each Peach Pear Plum*. New York: Viking, 1979.

Anderson, Hans Christian. *The Steadfast Tin Soldier*. New York: Harcourt Brace Jovanovich, 1992.

Bouchard, David. *My Little Pigs*. Winnipeg, Manitoba: Whole Language Consultants, 1991.

Brett, Jan. *The Mitten*. New York: Putnam, 1989.

Brown, Jeff. *Flat Stanley*. New York: Scholastic, 1974.

Calhoun, Mary. *Cross Country Cat*. New York: Mulberry, 1986.

————. *High-Wire Henry*. New York: Morrow Junior Books, 1991.

————. *Hot-Air Henry*. New York: Mulberry, 1986.

Celsi, Teresa. *The Fourth Little Pig*. Austin, TX: Steck-Vaughn, 1992.

Cherry, Lynne. *Who's Sick Today?* New York: Dutton, 1988.

Climo, Shirley. *The Egyptian Cinderella*. New York: Crowell, 1989.

Dodds, Dayle Ann. *Wheel Away!* New York: Scholastic, 1989.

Elting, Mary, and Folsom, Michael. *Q Is for Duck*. New York: Houghton Mifflin/ Clarion, 1980.

Gelman, Rita Golden. *Why Can't I Fly?* New York: Scholastic, 1976.

Hennessy, B.G. *The Missing Tarts*. New York: Scholastic, 1989.

Huck, Charlotte, and Lobel, Anita. *Princess Furball*. New York: Scholastic, 1989.

Lobel, Arnold. *Frog and Toad*. New York: Harper & Row, 1986.

Louie, Ai-Ling. *Yeh-Shen*. New York: Philomel, 1982.

Lowell, Susan. *The Three Little Javelinas*. Flagstaff, AZ: Northland Publishing, 1992.

Martin, Rafe, and Shannon, David. *The Rough-Face Girl*. New York: Putnam, 1992.

McMillan, Bruce. *One Sun*. New York: Scholastic, 1990.

Morrison, Bill. *Squeeze a Sneeze*. New York: Houghton Mifflin: 1977.

Oppenheim, Joanne, and Reid, Barbara. *Have You Seen Birds?* Scholastic: 1986.

Peet, Bill. *Chester the Worldly Pig*. New York: Houghton Mifflin, 1965.

———. *Cowardly Clyde*. New York: Houghton Mifflin, 1979.

———. *Cyrus the Unsinkable Sea Serpent*. New York: Houghton Mifflin, 1975.

———. *Hubert's Hair-Raising Adventure*. New York: Houghton Mifflin, 1959.

———. *Zella, Zack and Zodiac*. Boston: Houghton Mifflin, 1986.

Perrault, Charles. *Cinderella*. New York: Dial Books, 1985.

Raschka, Chris. *Yo! Yes?* New York: Orchard Books, 1993.

Sanibel Elementary School Third-Grade Students. *My Principal Lives Next Door*. Pinellas Park, FL: Willowisp Press, 1992.

Scieszka, Jon. *The Book That Jack Wrote*. New York: Viking, 1994.

———. *The True Story of the Three Pigs* (as told by A. Wolf). New York: Viking, 1989.

Slobodkina, Esphyr. *Caps for Sale*. New York: Harper & Row, 1968.

Steptoe, John. *Mufaro's Beautiful Daughters*. New York: Lothrop, Lee & Shepard, 1987.

Stow, Jenny (illustrator). *The House That Jack Built*. New York: Dial Books, 1992.

Strauss, Barbara, and Friedland, Helen. *See You Later Alligator*. Los Angeles: Price Stern Sloan, 1986.

Wood, Audrey. *Quick as a Cricket*. Clarkston, MI: Child's Play, 1982.

Young, Ed. *Lon Po Po*. New York: Philomel, 1989.

Plus these traditional stories:

Emperor's New Clothes, The
Little Red Riding Hood
Three Little Pigs, The

Poetry

DeRegniers, Beatrice S., ed. *Sing a Song of Popcorn: Every Child's Book of Poems*. New York: Scholastic, 1988.

Dunn, Sonja. *Butterscotch Dreams*. Markham, Ontario: Pembroke Publishers, 1987.

———. *Crackers & Crumbs*. Markham, Ontario: Pembroke Publishers, 1990.

Lee, Dennis. *Alligator Pie*. New York: Houghton Mifflin, 1975.

O'Neill, Mary. *Hailstones and Halibut Bones*. New York: Doubleday, 1961.

Prelutsky, Jack. *The New Kid on the Block*. New York: Greenwillow, 1984.

Silverstein, Shel. *Where the Sidewalk Ends*. New York: Harper & Row, 1974.

Professional Bibliography

Atwell, Nancie. *In the Middle: Writing, Reading and Learning with Adolescents.* Portsmouth, NH: Heinemann, 1987.

Calkins, Lucy. *Living Between the Lines.* Portsmouth, NH: Heinemann, 1991.

———. *The Art of Teaching Writing.* New Edition. Portsmouth, NH: Heinemann, 1994.

Cambourne, Brian, and Turnbill, Jan. *Coping With Chaos.* Portsmouth, NH: Heinemann, 1988.

Fletcher, Ralph. *What a Writer Needs.* Portsmouth, NH: Heinemann, 1993.

Forester, Anne D., and Reinhard, Margaret. *The Learners' Way.* Winnipeg: Peguis, 1989.

———. *The Teacher's Way.* Winnipeg: Peguis, 1994.

Gentry, J. Richard. *Spel . . . Is a Four-Letter Word.* Portsmouth, NH: Heinemann, 1994.

Gentry, J. Richard, and Gillet, Jean Wallace. *Teaching Kids to Spell.* Portsmouth, NH: Heinemann, 1993.

Graves, Donald H. *A Fresh Look at Writing.* Portsmouth, NH: Heinemann, 1994.

———. *Build a Literate Classroom.* Portsmouth, NH: Heinemann, 1991.

———. *Experiment With Fiction.* Portsmouth, NH: Heinemann, 1991.

———. *Explore Poetry.* Portsmouth, NH: Heinemann, 1992.

———. *Investigate Nonfiction.* Portsmouth, NH: Heinemann, 1989.

Hall, Nigel. *Writing with Reason.* Portsmouth, NH: Heinemann, 1989.

Harste, Jerome, and Short, Kathy. *Creating Classrooms for Authors.* Portsmouth, NH: Heinemann, 1988.

Lane, Barry. *After the End.* Portsmouth, NH: Heinemann, 1993.

Mooney, Margaret. *Reading To, With, and By Children.* Katonah, NY: Richard Owen, 1990.

Morrow, Lesley Mandel. *Literacy Development in the Early Years.* Englewood, NJ: Prentice-Hall, 1989.

Newkirk, Thomas, and Atwell, Nancie, eds. *Understanding Writing.* Portsmouth, NH: Heinemann, 1988.

Routman, Regie. *Invitations.* Portsmouth, NH: Heinemann, 1991.

———. *Transitions.* Portsmouth, NH: Heinemann, 1988.

Schlosser, Kristen G., and Phillips, Vicki L. *Building Literacy With Interactive Charts.* New York: Scholastic.

Schwartz, Susan, and Pollishuke, Mindy. *Creating the Child-Centred Classroom.* Katonah, NY: Richard Owen, 1991.

Strickland, Dorothy, and Morrow, Lesley Mandel. *Young Children Learn to Read and Write.* Newark, DE: International Reading Association, 1989.

Trelease, Jim. *The New Read-Aloud Handbook.* New York: Penguin, 1989.

———. *Hey! Listen to This: Stories to Read Aloud.* New York: Penguin, 1992.

Weaver, Constance. *Reading Process and Practice.* Portsmouth, NH: Heinemann, 1994.

Index

Index of Children's Literature and Traditional Stories

Index of Chants, Rhymes, and Poems